The RECRUITING SNITCH

Recruiting Secrets To Help Land Your Dream Job.

ALYSSE METZLER

Acknowledgement

As I write this acknowledgment I'm overwhelmed with pure joy. My friends, family, colleagues, business acquaintances, and some complete strangers helped me through the book writing process and it's impossible to recognize every individual who provided assistance. I would like to thank Elizabeth Toler and Goran Marich for seeing potential in me as a young lost college student needing career guidance and for providing me with challenges and opportunities I never thought imaginable. I would like to acknowledge Emily Sullivan for providing her unbiased opinion throughout the book writing process and being a constant enthusiast of my recruiting career. I would like to give special thanks to the cast and Executive Producer of Top Recruiter, The Competition. You have all become a huge support system in my life and a second family. I'm forever grateful for the constant motivation from Chris Lavoie, Mory Lavoie, Rayanne Thorn, Alex King, Kim Pope, Jude Martinez, Daniel Messemer, and the entire production team at C&I Studios. Thank you to the love of my life and best friend, Andre McFarline, for never allowing me to doubt myself or give up and for being my number one advocate. Thank you to Tina Critchfield, Annalisa Longo, Alana Henry, Trisha Fader, Katherine Douville, Sarah Hartman, Tara Rahaman, Chris Delaney, and Ryan Mattis for being true friends and who have been here for me throughout my career. Finally, words can't express how thankful I am for my family who provided me with lessons in life that made me who I am today and contributed in more ways than one to this book. Thank you to Brent, Lesley, Mom, and Dad for being with me every step of the way. Thank you to everyone for being with me through this journey, I dedicate this book to you.

TABLE OF CONTENTS

OVERVIEW

There are countless books about interviewing skills, résumé writing, and business etiquette. Reading these books, I sometimes wonder where the information came from. As I research, I realize it comes from educators, life coaches, human resources (HR) professionals, and other "credible" sources. Not one of these books was written by the people actually in the battlefield every day: the recruiters.

Wouldn't it be nice to know what recruiters ruminate on while they review your résumé?

Wouldn't it be cool to know what the recruiter is thinking while you sit in front of her on your interview?

How many times have you asked yourself, "Should I put that on my résumé or not? Should I talk about personal topics in an interview? What questions do I ask? What is the appropriate timeline for following up?"

Likewise, wouldn't it be nice to know what the other person is thinking while you are on your first date? Well, I can't help you with that, but getting a job is just like dating. So I'm here to let you into the mind of a recruiter. My fellow recruiters may think I'm a sellout, but I don't care. I want to help the unemployed get back to work. Once you understand how recruiters really think, you will understand the employment "game."

In the world of unemployment it's very easy to say, "I've done everything I can, but no one is hiring." I'm going to tell you right now to stop making that excuse! I've been recruiting for nine years now; do you know what that means? That means that for the past nine years, I've worked for corporations that are hiring! Yes, I said it: Companies are hiring left and right; you just haven't figured out how to get noticed. So today is the last day you should allow yourself to make that excuse. If you are unemployed, it's easy to sit back and collect unemployment. It's easy to get lazy and not apply, or not seriously look for a job.

Well, news flash—the longer you are unemployed, the worse you look to recruiters!

You need to treat job searching like a full-time job. Wake up Monday through Friday at 9:00 a.m. and get online. Take an hour off for lunch, and then get back to the computer. Do this every day until 5:00 p.m.

In preparation for this book, I didn't want to throw a bunch of outdated research and data at my readers. I wasn't interested in reporting the viewpoints of bloggers and people within the industry who have already published their opinions. I wanted to give you information directly from current recruiters within the United States.

I surveyed 101 recruiters who work for some of the largest corporations in the nation. Of the 101 recruiters surveyed, 70.3 percent are recruiters who work directly for corporations and 29.7 percent work in staffing agencies or firms. They represent more than fifty different industries, and are the people responsible for helping you find your next career. Throughout this book, I uncover the results from the survey and present direct quotes from these recruiters. I want to make sure you know I'm not just making this stuff up. I have 101 other recruiters agreeing with me and providing you with what they *really* think.

I give you specific real-life examples; including stories of mistakes applicants have made that destroyed their ability to get a job. Please do not think that you won't make these same mistakes, because I guarantee you that you will make them in your future, or that you have already made them in your past. Practice makes perfect, and knowledge is half the battle. So once you know what is *really* going on in the recruiters' heads, you will be able to ace the résumé review, get through the application process, impress the recruiter on your phone interview, wow the hiring manager in the face-to-face interview, and have a smooth and successful offer process.

So sit back and enjoy the wonderful world of recruiting.

CHAPTER 1

THE SECRET LIFE
OF A RECRUITER

....

"Being a recruiter is like working in a secret society. We are everywhere, and we can spot out other recruiters in a crowd; yet most people have no clue what it is we do all day. I love it."

BETH TOLER, SENIOR RECRUITER AND AVP

....

Most of the time, when I introduce myself to someone and tell them I'm a recruiter, I receive a blank stare and a follow-up question of, "Oh, interesting. So what are you recruiting for?"

My friends think I wine and dine people all day. My mom thinks I'm in executive meetings all day. Society thinks I'm a smooth-talking salesperson. My candidates think I'm sitting in my office counting the money I've made off of them. And *I* feel like I'm herding cats all day.

What do I really do?

I sit in my office in front of my computer, talk on the telephone, and make magic happen. A recruiter wears many hats, so the hat she was wearing when you met her likely will form your impression of *all* recruiters.

To help with this topic, I would like to explain the difference between a corporate recruiter and an agency recruiter or headhunter. Knowing the differences among the different types of recruiters will help you navigate the job-search process, so listen up.

Corporate recruiters are hired by companies that have constant turn-over *and* growth. In this instance, turnover is not a bad thing. Some companies hire contractors. Contractors are hired for a specific project and amount of time; they are not considered employees of the company they are contracting for. Because contractors are hired for specific projects for limited lengths of time, they are constantly ending their contracts, requiring backfills. Companies that have a lot of part-time positions experience turnover; they need to fill shifts because employees are working only twenty or fewer hours, yet their business is open for more hours. So companies that are fairly stable usually have a Department of Recruiters to help with the constant growth and to maintain staffing needs.

Corporate recruiters are more than likely paid a salary plus a yearly bonus based on their performance. Corporate recruiters are usually *not* a part of Human Resources. Yes, I know that is confusing, but most companies that hire recruiters want them to just do that one thing they are good at: *recruit*. So they are responsible for identifying and interviewing candidates, coordinating the entire interview process, extending and negotiating salaries, handling relocation details, and getting new employees set up for their first day of work. Then you know what happens? The new employees are then in the hands of the Human Resource Department. So now the recruiters can get back to doing what they love: *recruiting* and filling more positions.

The second type of recruiter you may come into contact with is the agency recruiter from a headhunting firm. This is someone who works for a staffing agency to help companies that may not have a recruiting department to find top talent. *You may want to consider using an agency or headhunting firm if you have not been successful in finding employment.* Each agency specializes in different industries. So, if you specialize in any of the following types of professions, I highly suggest that you research agencies in your area. These include careers in information technology, health care, engineering, sales, administrative positions, and accounting.

The agency recruiter works for an account manager, who acquires contracts set up with companies that don't have recruiting departments or have hard-to-fill openings. So the account manager will be in contact with companies the agency has built relationships with and receive job orders. The orders are open jobs, and if the agency can find the best candidate out there, then the company will pay the agency a fee. Using an agency shouldn't cost you, the candidate, anything.

If a company has a temporary job order, this means it is for a contractor job opening. Permanent job orders are for permanent job openings. So when you get a call from a recruiter who is "representing" a company, that normally means he or she is working for an agency or headhunter. The recruiter's job is to match a candidate to an open job order. An agency recruiter gets paid a salary and a commission per hire. Agencies will rake in anywhere from 10 to 40 percent of your base salary if they match you with a permanent job offer.

You are probably thinking, *why would I want to go to an agency if the principals are going to take so much of my salary?*

Here is a secret. Are you listening, or have I lost you already? Listen up! Many companies build into their budget the funds to pay an agency fee without it affecting what you will take home. So you will not notice the fee at all. That's right! You will still take home the salary you deserve for the role. The company has negotiated the fee already with the agency and is fully aware that it will cost a certain amount to use the agency's service. If an agency requires you to pay money out of your pocket I suggest that you go with another agency.

If an agency places you in a contract position, the agency will get paid a certain percentage of every hour you work. This is called a "contract-to-hire role" or a "contract position." Once you stop working, the agency will stop making money off of you. So they will do everything they can to keep you on the contract or to get another company lined up for you to work for when you are done.

Now that I've explained to you the differences among the types of recruiters out there, I'm back on track in explaining to you what a recruiter does all day. What is a recruiter's main responsibility? Here is the million-dollar answer: to fill job openings—period. That's it. That's what we get paid for.

I've conducted a survey of 101 recruiters in the United States. These recruiters came from both the corporate world and the agency world. I asked them: "On average, how many open positions are you working on at one time?"

The results indicated that 15.8 percent of them work on one to five job openings at one time, 25.7 percent work with six to ten openings, 12.9 percent work on eleven to fifteen openings, 21.8 percent work on sixteen to twenty openings, and 23.8 percent work on more than twenty openings at one time.

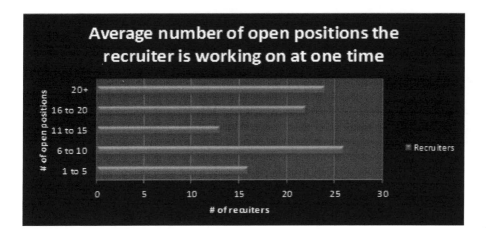

Yikes! As you can see, a typical recruiter has quite a few openings to fill at one time. As I mentioned above, we sometimes feel like we are herding cats all day. Really!

A typical recruiter will start the day off by taking a look at all of the new applicants who applied to her openings. She will go through the company's database and call on those who look like they have met the qualifications for the position. Next, she will conduct phone interviews to learn about the qualified applicants and present them to the hiring manager. If the hiring manager is interested in speaking with any of the candidates, the recruiter will then proceed with coordinating the interview process. From there, if the hiring manager is interested in hiring a candidate, the recruiter will put an offer together, extend it, and get the employee set up for his or her first day.

Sounds pretty simple, right? Not!

Here is what a recruiter accomplishes in one day in the *real* world:

- Reads and responds to more than sixty e-mails
- Has more than two hours of meetings with hiring managers
- Conducts about six phone interviews
- Speaks to maybe fifteen candidates to provide updates
- Consults with upset managers or employees (because people think that recruiting is HR, they tend to tell me all their problems, which I'm not qualified to handle).
- Screens more than fifty résumés
- Responds to five or more voice mails

And, oh, I forgot—sometimes we get to eat lunch.

The recruiter is the puppet master or the grand marshal of the parade, making sure everyone stays in their lane and remains calm while looking good doing it. Yeah, I said it—a recruiter must show no fear, exude confidence, be kind but assertive, solve problems, forecast issues, read people's minds, and—the best of all—remain cool and collected amid a cluster of problems.

Recruiters are extremely passionate people with type-A personalities. We are enthusiastic about the companies we work for, and we are obsessive about finding the best candidates for the companies we work for.

Here is another thing that may surprise you; are you ready? We want to hire you! We really do.

Seriously, everyone I interview, I genuinely want to see them succeed. Too often, though, either the candidate does something to mess up the opportunity or I realize I don't have the right opportunity to make them successful. I try to fit a round peg in a round hole, which is what creates the best future for my candidate and for my company. It's when recruiters try to fit a square peg in a round hole that issues arise both for the company and for the candidates.

I hope now you understand a little better what recruiters accomplish throughout their day and who we are in the scheme of this whole "how to get a job" thing. It's the important first step in your success.

CHAPTER 2

CAREER GOALS: WHAT DO YOU WANT IN LIFE?

"We are all searching for happiness and the 'ideal' job. I'm blessed to be in the position where I help people reach their goals and achieve the American dream."

ALAN ASHBY, SENIOR CORPORATE RECRUITER

W hat is your American dream? What does it mean to pursue your happiness?

We all have different dreams and goals in life. When you are searching for your next career move, you must identify what you are looking for in life and what steps you need to take to get them. If you work in a job that you are truly passionate about, you will never have worked a day in your life. Do you know how amazing that must feel? Work should not feel like work. You should not dread waking up every morning to go to work. Life is not about being miserable Monday through Friday and happy on the weekends. Your life is too short and precious to not be doing something daily that brings you happiness.

This chapter is about *your* truth, finding what it is that you really want in life, and how to go out and get it.

Why do people work?

To pay the bills, to afford things that they need to survive, to experience the things life has to offer, to contribute to society or to their families, and so on.

So here is the next question: Why do *you* work?

Your answer may be what I listed above, or it may be other reasons: to get out of the house, to be a partner with your husband or wife, to show your children how to make a living, to feel needed, to have a sense of accomplishment for your life, to please your parents, and so on.

There are so many reasons why you go to work, so the way you feel about your work should not be a negative feeling. By being happy and putting out positive energy in your daily work, you will breed other positive energy in your life, and you will accomplish things you never thought imaginable.

So, what are you passionate about? This is a time for you to self-reflect and to live in your truth. What God-given talents do you have? What activities do you enjoy? What are you doing when you find yourself the happiest? Take the time to think seriously about these questions, and *write down your answers*. This is the beginning of figuring out your path and how you can truly enjoy your work.

Some examples of things you may enjoy doing that can turn into a rewarding career are enjoying nature and the outdoors, or helping the elderly or children. If you love to shop, there is a job out there for you. If you are creative, if you are analytical and good with numbers, if you love meeting new people, if you love animals, if you like to solve difficult problems or love to travel, if you like to manage others, if you enjoy planning parties and events, if you like to play video games, and even if you like to go out to the local clubs and bars, guess what? There is a career path for you! That's right; all of these interests can turn into some great careers—even shopping. There are personal buyers out there, and corporate buyers who spend others' money to go shopping. If you like the night life, you can get into restaurant and bar management or even get into club promotion, in which case your job will be to party.

The lesson I want you to learn here is that you need to figure out what it is you enjoy doing, and then research and network to find out how to get a foot in the door.

In addition to whether they meet the qualifications for the job, I look for three things when interviewing my candidates: *personality, passion, and potential—the "Three P's."*

I asked 101 recruiters this question: "Have you hired someone who did not have the necessary experience but had a great personality, passion, and potential?"

The results are mind-altering. Of the 101 recruiters who completed the survey, 29 percent said, "No," and 71 percent said, "Yes."

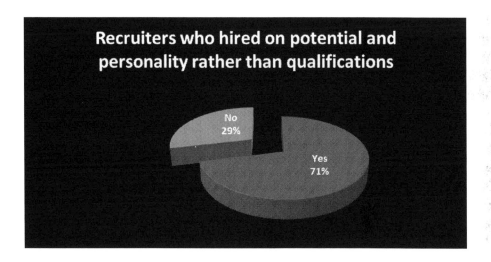

So how does this relate to you?

This means that if you are *passionate* about something, you are more likely to get the job over someone who is qualified but may not have the right passion or potential. This also means that you should not be discouraged if you don't have a lot of experience in the field you want to work in. You have to start somewhere. So remember the "three P's" when looking for your next career move: *personality, passion, and potential.*

We are all in search of the American dream. If everyone could achieve the American dream, it would not be called a dream; it would be called the "American reality."

What is your dream?

I will tell you right now, if your dream is based on making money, then, my friend, you are in for a rude awakening. An inexperienced person may say, "I don't care where I work; I just want to make a lot of money."

I interviewed a previous coworker whose salary exceeds $250K a year and who seems to be living the "American dream." I asked him if he was happy.

He responded by saying, "Happy? Hmmm, great question. Let's see, I travel 75 percent of the month, so I see my family exactly seven days a month. I work ten or more hours a day with very few breaks. I missed the births of both of my children because I was working, and I miss all of my kids' school events and milestones in their lives. My responsibilities at work require me to drastically change people's lives, and sometimes it's not for the best. I can't sleep at night without a sleep aid because I have so much guilt in my head. I've gained fifty pounds in the last two years because of my stress. I'm on medication for high blood pressure, and I'm almost certain my wife is cheating on me. So am I happy? I don't think I've felt genuine happiness in ten years."

I then asked him if he could go back in time and change his career path, what he would change it to.

After his previous response, I really wasn't shocked when he said, "If I could go back, I would have listened to my eight-year-old self who wanted to swim with dolphins and be out on the beach all day. I would have gone to school for marine biology, traveled the oceans, and helped save marine life. Man, that was an awesome dream I had, and I totally could have done it. Instead, I got into the business world and chased the almighty dollar, leaving me with nothing but an empty feeling."

Money does not buy happiness, and if you are choosing a career only because it will make you a lot of money, then please put this story in the front of your memory. This executive I interviewed said, "I would rather make forty-five thousand dollars a year if it meant I would be home every night for dinner, period." Think about it.

Remember my saying in the beginning of this chapter: "If you work in a job that you are truly passionate about, you will never have worked a day in your life"?

Don't spend your entire life *pursing* happiness; spend your life *experiencing* happiness by doing what you love. I hope you don't ever look back and say you wished you had listened to your eight-year-old self.

Your new American dream should be to not work a day in your life.

CHAPTER 3

About Those Gaps in Your Employment History

"During the gap of unemployment on your résumé, you say you were a 'consultant.'

We know what that means...."

DENNY VOYLES, RECRUITING MANAGER

I know it sounds brutal, and yes, you may have been an actual consultant or entrepreneur. If that is the case, be ready to show your LLC tax information or statement of income from your "consultant" work.

On the same survey I conducted, I asked the recruiters the following question: "When someone leaves a job without another lined up, do you consider that a red flag?"

The responses were pretty straightforward. Of the 101 surveys completed, 8 percent of the respondents said, "Not at all," 23 percent said, "Yes, majorly," and 69 percent said, "Sometimes, if they don't have a good reason."

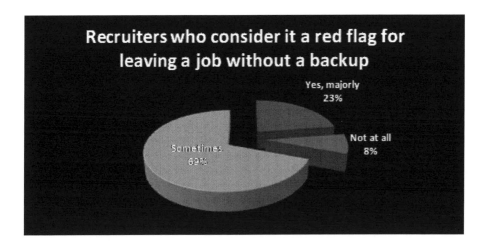

So the lesson for you in this study is to try not to leave a job without having something else lined up, since 92 percent of recruiters may feel it's a red flag, period.

I would like to make a point prior to plunging into this chapter that is exceptionally important. We all know that we currently live in a day and age in which it is acceptable to have had three to four jobs in the past eight years. I'm aware that staying with one company until retirement, like our parents or grandparents did, is no longer the norm. I understand that companies are merging, acquiring, and downsizing. So if you have been laid off due to a company closing or budget cuts, that is acceptable, and I will not hold that against you.

So now that you know this, don't try to candy-coat your résumé by fudging on the dates or lying.

When a candidate says he was laid off due to x, y, and z reasons, you'd better believe I'm researching that company. I would say that 90 percent of the time a company goes through a layoff, it makes the news, and I can confirm the dates. So if you were fired and just told me you were "laid off," but nowhere do I see that your company went through any sort of downsizing or layoffs, I know you are misrepresenting.

In this chapter, I analyze some of the most common responses I've heard from applicants about why they left their jobs and tell you what I'm really thinking when I hear it. Get ready for some reality to come your way.

When I was interviewing a candidate who had a two-year gap in her employment, I inquired about it. She communicated to me a story of how she felt stuck in her position and was not inspired or challenged. She said she decided to leave her job to pursue a dream of owning her own salon. I responded by saying, "That's awesome! I like to see people pursuing their dreams."

Here is what was *really* going on in my mind. I thought, *she left a job where she was earning fifty thousand dollars a year plus benefits, which was a nice, comfortable way of life*. I assumed she had money already saved to put in this investment. I assumed she had a business plan and had executed part of the plan. I expected that she'd had a location and had been ready to start the business. With these thoughts in my head, I inquired further.

Through my probing, I found out that she did not have any money to put into the company. She was working part-time babysitting for a family friend. She was turned down by a few banks for a business loan, and so she just stopped pursing her dream. She was then living in debt, had to sell her home, and ended up getting a divorce.

So what did I learn? I discovered that she was fired from her company and tried to candy-coat the situation by making herself sound like an entrepreneur. This situation occurs more often than you would believe. The stories are all different, but the conclusion is *always* the same—that the person was terminated, for a particular reason.

The moral of this story is to be honest and try not to have anything more than a four-month gap in employment. Even if you take a job that isn't exactly what you want at the time, take it. You can always keep looking, but at least you have income and something to show for what you have been doing with your time.

I approve of people venturing off into owning their own businesses or working as consultants. Here is the key: *Do not quit your current job* to do it until you are 100 percent ready and able to start the business within two months.

This means you have saved all the money you need, or have received the approvals for a loan. You have a location and a lease ready to be signed and you have all of the contracts or licenses set up, etc. In our economy, the average time it takes to find employment is five months. So keep in mind, if you quit your job, and your business is not ready to take off within your first one to two months of unemployment, you may be out of a job for five months or more. Be realistic with your goals and know when the right time to quit your job is and when to stick it out.

Another reason I see gaps in employment is due to people pursuing a college education. In chapter 13, I offer information for recent college graduates. In this case, I'm discussing people who have work experience, stop working for two to four years to pursue a college degree, and then want to get back into their field.

Here's the brutal truth: That will *not* help you.

Recruiters will look at that as time you spent *not* getting experience. You may have learned a bunch of relevant information for the job, but learning and doing are totally different. So that gap you took will set you back, not thrust you forward as I'm sure your professors and college advisors told you. The best way to handle this situation is to *not quit* your job. If this means working full-time and then going to school online or on the weekends or evenings, then do that. Keep working and gain experience while learning. Recruiters will look at that as ambition, and will want to invest in you for job openings. If we see that you quit a stable job to go back to school, we think you may have lost your marbles. That is the truth.

In summary, if you are looking to pursue higher education, then please do; just keep your job while doing so.

Another situation you may have run into in your career is having the dreadful thought: *I can't stand working here anymore; I'm going to quit*.

We have all worked in unbearable situations, with horrible managers, annoying coworkers, never-pleased clients, stressful meetings, and long hours. You may have had it when it comes to where you work, to the point where you just want to quit. Unless you are being mentally abused, harassed, or harmed in any way, *then you must not quit without another job lined up*.

When an applicant tells me she quit her job because the people she worked with were snobbish, or her manager was unpleasant, or the work environment was unbearable, then I think, *well, now she wakes up every day not knowing where to find a job, she has no income coming into the family, and she is in debt*. So is the situation she was in while working worse than what she is in now? Most of the time, it is not. At least she had a job to go to every day to provide for her family.

Instead of vacating a job you may not enjoy due to some of the circumstances I just listed, try to change the circumstances. Speak to someone in HR, talk to your manager, and address things with your coworkers. If that still does not work, then take control of your own ability to deal with difficult people and situations. Try breathing exercises, meditating, praying, or seek counseling. Do things to get yourself through the day.

Of course, there are things you cannot change, so in that case suck it up while you look for another job.

By keeping your current job while looking for another, you should have the ability to handle the negative things going on in your current situation. Just keep in mind that it's almost over.

As a recruiter, when someone tells me he quit his job because he couldn't take it anymore, I immediately ask, "Did you do anything to try to change what was bothering you at work?"

This question will show me a lot about this candidate. I want to hire someone who has the ability to address issues in the workplace, someone who tries to better the workplace, someone who is proactive regarding problems in the work environment, someone who takes action, and most of all, someone who is not a quitter just because times got tough. If you quit your job without another lined up, then please be prepared to explain the situation, what you did to try to overcome it, and what you planned on accomplishing in your life by quitting.

Another common reason people give for having gaps in their résumé is that they took time off for personal or family issues. This is a touchy topic and covers a lot of different types of cases. Some of those cases include divorces, deaths, sicknesses, accidents, and issues surrounding children. I'm fully aware that these things happen in lives. People handle these cases differently and require different lengths of time to recover from the issue. It's when the length of time seems to exceed the assumed time needed to handle the personal situation that raises red flags to recruiters.

My main concern is when people take off longer than three months for "family" or "personal" reasons. If you had to quit your job to take care of a family member who was sick and you have been unemployed for more than three months, the main question I have is, *I wonder if the person whom you were taking care of wanted you to quit your job, lose opportunities in the future, and become his or her personal nurse?*

I'm assuming the person who you are taking care of would still want you to achieve your goals and be able to provide for yourself. If there is a way to keep your job while helping out a family member who needs you, then please keep your job. If you cannot work, then please make sure you have something in place after three months so that you can return to work. Before you care for someone else, you need to care for yourself.

I'm normally understanding about these situations, and you are welcome to discuss the situation in as much or as little detail as you feel comfortable. Please do not give too much information to your recruiter. There are some things we do not want to know. We do not need to know how your husband was controlling and all about your sticky divorce. Just say, "I had to take some time off while settling a divorce." That is enough information for us to know why you have a gap in your employment.

Finally, I speak to many women and men who took time off to be stay-at-home parents. I think that is amazing and I don't blame them for wanting to spend time with their children. The one thing I encourage stay-at-home parents to do is to try to work part-time or volunteer. It's also helpful to take courses or attend seminars to keep your skills sharp. It saddens me when parents stay home for six years and don't do anything to maintain their skills or expertise. In those six years people in their industry have been learning new skills, sharpening their knowledge, learning new technologies, getting promoted, and networking.

If you take the time off and don't continue attending networking events or doing anything to keep your skills sharp, you will fall back in your career tremendously and all the hard work you put in before you had your bundles of joy will have gone in vain.

If you have a gap like this and are just returning to the work life then please don't expect to jump right back in at the same level you left. You may have to take a part-time job first or a contract. You may have to take a huge pay decrease and work your way back up. The shorter your time off, the better chances you have to get your career back up and running.

I've touched on gaps in employment due to a company layoff, merger, or acquisition; pursuing your dream of entrepreneurship; pursuing higher education; tending to family and personal issues; and staying at home with your children. I hope I've shed some light on acceptable and unacceptable reasons for gaps in your résumé.

Below are actual quotes from recruiters across the United States who completed my survey. I asked them to tell me what secrets they would like to share with the unemployed. Here are the comments that relate to the topic discussed in this chapter.

- "Unemployment occurs, especially in this economy. Potential employers understand that, but most companies still desire those who have been unemployed to be either pursuing education or professional training/development *while looking for new positions*."
- "Don't go over one year of being unemployed. The more of a gap, the harder it is for the third-party recruiting firm to help. Not a good idea since third-party recruiting firms can probably get your résumé in front of a hiring manager more effectively than you can by applying on your own."
- "Be honest about what you know and honest about what you don't know. Lying will get you nowhere."
- "Volunteer to show that you are doing something other than sitting at home. Put that experience on your résumé. Get LinkedIn." (We will be discussing social media in chapter six.)
- "Do something—school, contract work, volunteerism—rather than just job search for too long a period of time."
- "A significant gap in employment can make employers think there is an issue. Always find legitimate ways to keep your résumé active, like volunteering or self-employment."
- "Volunteer to mark time on your résumé."

CHAPTER 4

THE LABELS WE SECRETLY ASSIGN YOU

"One of my biggest pet peeves with candidates is when they hound me. Applicants don't realize that things don't always move quickly within the company. It doesn't mean you didn't get the job or that you have been overlooked. It just means we are busy, that's all."

ANONYMOUS, CORPORATE RECRUITER

I was speaking to my brother years ago and venting to him about my lack of success in my dating life. He broke the "guy code" by telling me that men have labels for all of their lady friends, and I may have obtained the "Just a Friend" label without even being aware of it.

He said women put themselves in these classes based on how they conduct themselves. Some are fun to stay at home and relax with. Some are good to be around because they can cook. Some are wife material. Some are very pretty and are good to show off around their friends, and some are really fun just for the moment but there isn't a future, and so on. He informed me that men put labels on all of their female friends, and once they're in a certain category, it is hard to get out.

So just like I had no clue that men immediately put me in a "category," you have no clue that recruiters are classifying their candidates. You may be scratching your head at this one, thinking, *I didn't know there were different types of applicants*. This chapter unlocks some recruiting secrets and how we may be labeling you without your knowing. I wanted to uncover this topic so that you can identify which type of applicant you are and solve some problems you may be having finding employment.

THE JACK-OF-ALL-TRADES / THE SERIAL APPLIER

I'm all about persistence and agree that you should apply to job openings that you are interested in. However, I have a difficult time understanding applicants who apply to *all* of the openings I post. The Serial Applier will apply to all of my openings, thinking they are qualified for them all. As mentioned in chapter 5, please only apply to roles where you feel you have met the minimum qualifications. If you are a Serial Applier, please stop wasting your time. It gets to the point where recruiters recognize certain names and immediately disqualify them because we feel you do not truly know what you want to do and have wasted our time and your time by applying to literally all of our openings.

Here is why it is annoying: We have to click on *every single* application that comes through our job boards. So if you have applied to fifty openings, we have to click on your profile or name fifty times. Not fun.

Most people who are Serial Appliers are also The-Jack-of-all-Trades applicants. These are people who have a lot of experience doing very random things. They do not have a specialty in one thing or a niche, so they feel they can do any job posted. My advice is to find a niche, find a skill that you are good at, and become an expert at it. I'd rather see an expert in one or two fields than an entry-level person who has experience in many fields.

THE DESPERATE

At the end of my survey, I asked the recruiters, "What is your biggest pet peeve with candidates?"

Many of the comments were around The Desperate applicant. There is a fine line between excitement and desperation. Just like in a relationship, many relationships end up failing when one person becomes needy, annoying, too demanding, and overbearing.

Recently, an applicant figured out our e-mail alias at my current company, and he e-mailed fifteen people saying that he had applied to a position and how excited he was about the possibility of working here. Do you know what those fifteen recipients did to that e-mail they received from this applicant? They forwarded to me. So not only did I have the person apply to my opening, but then I had fifteen of the *same exact* e-mails come to me from fifteen different people in my company. What was funny about this situation is that this applicant was very qualified, and I had already forwarded his résumé to my hiring manager. We did end up hiring this person, but not because he e-mailed fifteen of our employees; we hired him because he was the most qualified for the position. Please don't spam a company while trying to get a job; it will not help you in your venture to be employed there.

THE WEEKLY AMBASSADOR

The Weekly Ambassadors are those who have already interviewed and now call me on a weekly basis to see if I have anything else for them. They may also be those candidates who are currently in the interview process and call to check on the status every week or more frequently. These types of applicants have taken the idea of following up to a whole new level. When I tell someone, "I will give you a call as soon as I have news one way or the other," that means I will call you when I know something. If you do not hear from me, that means I don't have any more news for you.

So you may now wonder when the right time to follow up is.

If you have not heard anything from your recruiter after a week, I recommend sending an e-mail or making one phone call to follow up. As mentioned in chapter one, 58.5 percent of recruiters are working on eleven or more openings at one time. This means that if I work a typical forty-hour week and have eleven openings, I have fewer than four hours a week to focus on each position. Our time is very limited, and we may, in fact, have intentions to call you to follow up but may have been pulled in other directions. So a follow-up is appreciated, but nothing more than that is needed.

THE STALKER

The next type of applicant is a fun one, and you may be thinking, *No way do people actually do this*. Well, I'm here to tell you that it happens all the time. This applicant is known as none other than The Stalker. These applicants are Stalkers during the interview process and afterward. They friend-request me on Facebook, follow me on Twitter, call me many times in a row but do not leave voice mails, and e-mail me to "just say hello." Please keep in mind that your relationship with a recruiter should be professional. It is acceptable to connect with your recruiter on LinkedIn; however, all other social media sites should be off-limits.

Second, if you plan on calling a recruiter, please leave a voice mail if she does not pick up. Do not call her back until she responds to your voice mail. It is frustrating when someone calls numerous times in a row and does not leave a message. It is also not acceptable to call, leave a message, and then continue to call. This is business etiquette 101, so please ingrain this lesson in your head.

THE PASSIVE

The next type of applicant is the Passive applicant. Passive applicants are candidates who did not directly apply to my opening or reach out to me directly. This type of applicant is happy in his current role and is not looking for other opportunities. These are awesome people, and I actively seek them out for my openings. I receive information from my professional network about people who are doing a great job and to whom I should be reaching out.

Passive candidates are the most difficult for a recruiter to recruit but usually end up being the best hires because they have proven abilities recognized by their peers. Passive candidates hold the power because I called them. Your goal in your career is to do such a great job in your current role that word travels within your industry and you have recruiters, like me, calling you for their opportunities. If you become a subject-matter expert and an overall irreplaceable employee, you should never be without a job. Your goal is to become a Passive candidate.

THE ACTIVE

On the flip side of the Passive candidate, we have the Active candidate. I'm assuming that most of you reading this book are Active candidates. Active candidates actively apply to job openings and are seeking employment. They are highly engaged in the interview process and genuinely want the positions I'm hiring for. It's easier to recruit an Active candidate because they applied to my roles. The rules are a little different for Active and Passive candidates. An Active candidate must remain easy to reach, maintain a positive attitude throughout the interview process, and really prove that he is the best person for the job.

THE GHOST

The next type of candidate is called the Ghost. The best way to explain this candidate is to fill you in on a real-world Ghost I encountered this past year. This person, whom I will call Bill, was interviewing for a niche position. This meant that my company needed someone with very specific experience and a much focused skill set. Only a handful of people in the industry have those skills. Bill had these skills, so he phone-interviewed with a few managers and me. The feedback from his phone interviews was very positive, and my hiring manager wanted to fly him to town for an on-site interview to meet with the rest of the team. I called him to let him know the good news.

Guess what? He did not pick up. Days went by, and I left numerous messages but received no callback. Yes, I was disappointed and felt that my team and I had wasted a lot of time. We ended up moving on and forgot that the whole thing happened. Six months later, I received an e-mail from an employee I work with saying that Bill was interested in a different position that I had opened. You can imagine my thoughts at that time. I thought, *Oh! No way! Why would I want to waste my time again? Why would I even want to talk to him? What will the team think when they hear that Bill is interviewing again for another position? This is going to make me look really bad. Nope, I'm not going to even cross this bridge. He had his chance, and he ruined it.* Those were my exact thoughts. If a recruiter has these thoughts about you, then your chances of getting a job at that company are slim to none, my friend.

The Ghost is someone who starts off the interview process well and then just disappears. They are active candidates who have expressed interest in my role. I may talk to these candidates a couple of times and may even fly them in for on-site interviews. Then when it comes time to make things official, they disappear. Ladies, I'm sure you can relate this to some of your ex-boyfriends.

This type of candidate is just testing the waters, seeing what's out there, but is not ready to commit to any openings. I believe it is important to never turn down an interview. Practicing your interview skills is important, and you should attend any interview that is offered to you (any interview that is local to you), even if you are not 100 percent sure that you want the position you are interviewing for.

Ghost candidates immediately build a negative reputation with the recruiter and even the managers with whom they may have interviewed. We feel that Ghosts waste everyone's time, and we believe there is no excuse for not calling a recruiter back. The Ghost has burned all bridges for any future employment opportunities at the company. The main lesson here is to not become a Ghost candidate.

If, in the middle of the interview process, you realize that the job or company is not for you, then please pick up the phone and call the recruiter to let her know. I respect anyone who calls me directly and tells me they are pulling themselves out of the interview process. I'll also be more than happy to keep them in mind for a different role in the future. Please have respect for your recruiter and call her back. Don't become a Ghost. You never know when you may need that recruiter or want to join her company.

THE SUPERSTAR

I'm going to end this chapter with my ideal candidate, the Superstar. These candidates follow the interview process seamlessly and are very easy to work with. They respond to my calls or e-mails, they are easy to talk to, they are positive, they are not difficult, and they follow the correct "rules" during the interview process.

I've noticed something in common among all of my Superstar applicants: They connect with me on a personal level. It's nice when they tell me some things about themselves beyond the interview questions. It is important for me to connect with each candidate in some manner, and the best way to relate to me is to talk about something personal. Feel free to tell your recruiter some things you like to do in your personal life, and to talk about what you are passionate about outside of getting the job you are interviewing for. I've noticed that my conversations with those candidates who have opened up to me are a lot easier and more candid. So this is a great secret to becoming a Superstar applicant—open up.

Now, I feel the urge to put in a public service announcement on behalf of every recruiter out there. As mentioned above, getting personal is a great way to connect with your recruiter; however, there is a fine line between some information and too much information.

We do not need to know about all of the drama in your life. We don't need to know how stressed out you are, how sick you are feeling, how you and your significant other on are on the rocks, etc. I've had candidates open up to me on a whole other dimension, and it made me feel sorry for them and extremely uncomfortable—not to mention the fact that it made them look like a flight risk. So it's OK to talk about positive things going on in your life like birthdays, anniversaries, trips planned, projects you are working on, goals you have in your personal life, or your holiday plans, but keep it on that level.

At the end of the survey I conducted, I asked the following question: "What is your biggest pet peeve with candidates, and what advice do you have for the unemployed?"

I copied the responses below from the survey. To maintain data integrity, I did not edit the *content* of the comments collected; I only edited grammatical and punctuation of the responses. So here are the responses relating to the topic discussed in this chapter. Hear it straight from the "horse's mouth," as they say.

- "Constantly calling to 'check on the status.'" (aka the Weekly Ambassador)
- "When they are hard to get ahold of after you've both discussed moving forward. In other words, when they fall off the face of the earth! Flaky…" (aka the Ghost)
- "Applying for multiple positions that are totally different from each other. I want to see that someone is looking for a career, not just a job to pay the bills." (aka the Serial Applier or Jack-of-all-Trades)
- "They express interest in working and then they disappear, or they get the job they've always wanted and then start asking for time off, schedule changes, the ability to work on their own time, etc." (aka the Ghost)
- "Calling continually after they don't get a job to see if I have anything else for them."(aka the Weekly Ambassador)
- "Candidates that think they are great matches for all the positions I have posted!" (aka Jack-of-all-Trades)
- "Lack of follow-up or being too aggressive in following up." (aka the Ghost or the Weekly Ambassador)
- "Not responding in a timely manner." (Follow up within twenty-four hours.)
- "The ones who e-mail me constantly. It just annoys me. I appreciate follow-up (especially because I'm bad with it), but there is a line between e-mailing me daily when I told you I don't have an update, and keeping in touch passively (once every week or two weeks)." (aka the Weekly Ambassador or the Desperate)
- "Acting desperate is a big red flag. You have to convey that you want the job you are applying for, not just any job." (aka the Desperate)
- "Please don't send your résumé and then follow up with a phone call thinking it's going to make you stand out, because it's not; it only annoys me. You will find a job, so stay positive—recruiters can tell when you're disgruntled, and it's a major turnoff."(aka the Desperate)

CHAPTER 5

THE SCIENCE OF A JOB DESCRIPTION

"One of my biggest frustrations is 'Serial Appliers,' candidates who apply to everything, even if they don't meet the minimal qualifications. It's like they didn't even read my job description. Why do they think we even post a job description?"

ANONYMOUS, CORPORATE RECRUITER

That's right, another secret for you: Recruiters have zero tolerance for "Serial Appliers".

I spend a lot of time creating job descriptions to clearly advertise the position and what we are looking for. So when I have candidates who apply to everything I post, I automatically get frustrated. Agitating a recruiter is *not* how you get a job.

Before I get into the job descriptions, I would like to inform you of job posting policies. Normally, large corporations have pretty strict posting policies. This means that a position *must* be posted externally (meaning that it is posted for anyone to see on the Internet) for a certain period of time, allowing external candidates time to apply. This is a legal policy set in place to protect you. So what does this mean to you?

This means that sometimes when you see a position posted, the company may already have an internal candidate in mind; however, they are open to seeing if there is a better suited external candidate. The job has been posted for the required period of time, allowing all external applicants a fair chance at applying for the position before the recruiter looks internally. So this is why you may see postings up for such a short period of time. They were never really planning on recruiting for it; they just posted it because they had to. Don't get discouraged; just keep it moving and respect that the company looks out for their internal employees.

Now, let's look at how you can become one of those internals.

A good job description consists of four parts: company overview, job overview, job requirements, and preferred skills. The company overview and job overview are normally templates created by the company or recruiter, so those are pretty plain and straightforward. The parts you need to focus on are the *job requirements* and the *preferred skills*.

The requirements are usually direct and easy to gauge or prove, like years of experience (we can add your years of direct experience from your résumé) or education level (we can verify your diplomas and degrees). If you do not have those requirements, please do not apply.

The problematic part is when a company requires soft skills, like strong communication, attention to detail, ability to multitask, working well in a team environment, etc. Those are all skills that we can't tell from your résumé; however, you'd better believe we will ask you about those skills during your interview. If a job description states that you must work well with people in a team environment but you know for a fact you like to work independently and, not on a team, do not apply. You will set yourself up to fail and will waste your time and the recruiter's time.

Whenever I receive a new opening to fill, I always start by meeting with my hiring manager and putting together a job description to be posted. We take the time to discuss their "must-haves" and their "preferred-to-haves." This is just like dating; we all have our list of criteria we *must* see in a partner and our criteria we would *like* to see. So, for example, if you know you do not want to date someone who smokes cigarettes, but only smokers are asking you out, you are going to get pretty frustrated. That is the same way I feel about applicants who apply to my jobs without meeting the minimum qualifications; they are wasting my time.

When I put together a job description, I am putting together a formula for a successful employee. I'm advertising to you what I must see and what I would like to see. Think how easy dating would be if we could just advertise exactly what we are looking for. So if you do not meet the must-haves or requirements of the job, please do not apply.

Now, you may think, *Well, I just want to try to see what happens*.... Here I am being a mind reader; I know what is going to happen—*nothing*. Please listen to this tip and save us both time and energy.

Before you get on the Internet to look up openings, do some soul searching. Write down what type of work you are looking for. Have a goal in mind of what industry and what type of work will make you happy and successful. Do not just jump online and start to apply! I repeat, *do not just jump online and start to apply!* Research your industry, look up companies that are growing and expanding, talk to your friends and family about what they do and where they work, *and* finish reading this book first!

From there, get a list of ten companies you want to work for and a list of five positions you would be good at. Then target those companies and take a look at what they have opened. Read the job descriptions and apply only to those that meet your current career goals and for which you meet at least the minimum qualifications.

CHAPTER 6

SOCIAL MEDIA

"I was doing some social media research on a potential sales hire that had an exceptional background. I came across her Facebook page and her newsfeed was riddled with negative comments about her current employer, personal complaints about her life, and overall nagging issues. I was impressed with her resume, but did not bring her in for an interview due to the fact that she was so publicly negative about everything in her life. Negativity breeds negativity, therefore I wouldn't even consider bringing her in for an interview."

ALEX KING, RECRUITING AND STAFFING DIRECTOR

C urrently, social media have taken over most of our lives. Nothing is private anymore, and anyone can find out anything about you if they put in the time and effort. Everything you post is permanently put on the World Wide Web and will be a part of your life forever. Even if you delete a picture or post, you have created a footprint that can be accessed.

In the survey, I asked recruiters the following question: "Do you look up your candidates on Facebook/Twitter and/or Google their name?"

The responses were as expected, but may be a shocker to you. Of the 101 recruiters who responded, only 30 percent said, "No, never," while 52 percent said, "Sometimes," and 18 percent said, "Yes, all the time."

I'm not risking anything, so let's assume the majority of "sometimes" responses were "yes."

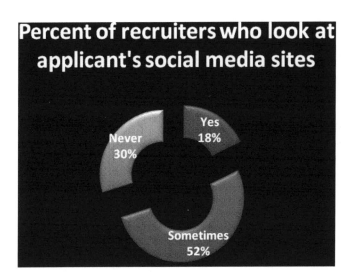

This means that you have a 70 percent chance that a recruiter is look- ing at your social media profiles or searching Google for your name when you apply to their job or are interviewing. Yes, that is correct. I know you can't change what you have already posted, but I'm here to tell you now that the things you post from here on must be positive and professional.

You may be thinking, *what I do in my personal life and on my personal social media sites is no one's business*. Yes, you are right, to an extent. However, the moment you post something on social media, you have made it everyone's business by putting your life out there for anyone to judge you on, period. It's not right, and it's not fair, but it's a fact of life, and you need to accept it.

Here is something else to remember: Legally, a recruiter cannot make a hiring decision based on your social-media activities. So now you are wonder- ing, *"Then why do recruiters look, and why are you telling me to be careful?"*

I'm telling you this because even though we cannot legally make a decision based on social media, we are human, and it may sway how we feel about you as a candidate for our opening. Why would my company want to invest in you as an employee if I visit your Facebook page and see you half-dressed in all your photos, drinking alcohol, partying every night, speaking profanities, venting about how so and so broke your heart, and so on?

When I was a junior in college, I worked directly under a CEO for a very successful mortgage company. During my second week on the job, he called me into his office and said, "I understand you are in college, and you are twenty years old. However, you have a professional job now and are required to be here every day from 9:00 a.m. until 5:00 p.m. You are required to be polished and professional like everyone else, and your age will not be a factor in the mistakes you make. Your personal life will affect your performance, so from here on out, I want you to analyze who you hang out with, who you talk to on the phone, and what you do when you are not in the office—and *if* the people you hang around are not in the same boat as you, then you need to cut them out of your life. This is the time in your life when the people you hang out with either rise to the occasion or you just leave them in the dust."

His comment hit me pretty hard. This was *before* MySpace and Facebook, so I wasn't advertising anything negative. I can only imagine how college students are nowadays with their personal activities and postings. I did take his advice and started to realize that the people I was hanging around were not doing anything with their lives. They went out five nights a week, slept all day, and were dramatic about stupid things that really didn't matter in life. I started to not go out as much, and I started to distance myself from certain people. I soon realized that I had been provided an once-in-a-lifetime opportunity, and if I didn't step up and raise above all the other college students, I might regret it in the future.

Lo and behold, he promoted me within one month. I was earning $35K plus commission as a college student. The company was growing, so he needed help hiring his mortgage originators. He called on me to help double his staff. That is how I started my recruiting career. The moral of the story is that your personal life *does* affect your professional life, so stop putting junk on your social-media profiles for everyone to see.

The first thing you need to do when you are applying for jobs is to go on all of your social-media sites and check the privacy settings. Make sure everything is set on private and nothing is public. Remember, your profile pictures are *always* public, so make sure the pictures you choose to represent your profile are in good taste. Next, please go in and delete any pictures that show you partaking in any subjective activities. If you are twenty-one years of age or older, you may not think having pictures of you drinking alcoholic beverages is discriminating; however, keep the number of pictures to a minimum. I don't want to see you getting drunk in every picture.

Second—this is mostly for ladies, but men do it, too. Please delete any pictures in which you are not wearing appropriate clothing. You should be fully clothed unless you are at the pool or a beach. I don't want to see you making flirty pictures with your shirt off in your bathroom. I don't want to see you in sexual positions, and I don't want to see you in clothes showing your stomach, thighs, or butt. I'm amazed at the number of women who put their bodies out on the Internet for everyone to see. They are objectifying themselves, and it shows that they have zero respect for themselves and low self-esteem. Would you walk into an interview with a miniskirt and a low-cut shirt on? I hope not....

Finally, delete any posts in which you are using any type of profanity. People who use profanity show a lack of professionalism and seem uneducated because they can't find another word to use besides a swear word. This is for men and women. Mature and professional people do not swear, period.

In summary, check your privacy settings, edit your pictures, and audit your postings. By taking these steps, you are prohibiting yourself from being poorly judged by a future employer.

We cannot run from the fact that people are looking at our social-media profiles. We cannot change what we have posted in the past; however, we can change what we post from here on out.

I'm not asking you to keep from partaking in the social-media frenzy. I'm telling you to be smarter about it. Use social media for networking, keeping in touch with friends and family, announcing good things in your life, and sharing knowledge. Social media should not be used to objectify yourself, vent about all the issues in your life, push your political or religious beliefs, or brag about how cool you may think you are. Your personal life should *not* be on the Internet. There are certain things that need to remain personal.

You have a 70 percent chance of a future employer looking at your profile. If you are not willing to share it with a prospective employer, then don't share it at all.

CHAPTER 7

Résumé Writing 101

"A poorly written résumé infuriates me. A résumé tells me so much about a candidate. How do people expect an interview or a job if their résumé isn't on point?"

KATHERINE DOUVILLE, SENIOR RECRUITER

Résumé writing is most likely the most dreadful task to take on when you are unemployed. This is even scarier if you've never had to write one before. I hope that, after reading this chapter, you are more confident about how to get the ball rolling.

Your résumé is your advertisement for yourself. How much time do you spend looking at advertisements in magazines? Well, I hate to tell you this, but in the survey, I asked the recruiters, "On average, how much time do you spend looking at a single résumé when you are sourcing for your openings?"

You are going to learn a lot from these results, which concluded that 74.2 percent of the recruiters stated that they look at a résumé for only *one minute or less*.

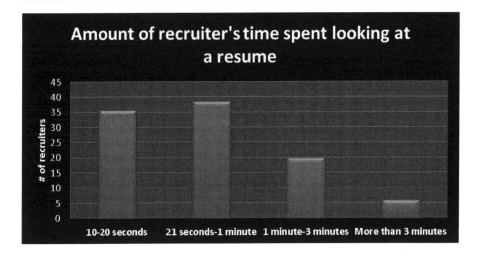

Yikes! So, basically, seven out of ten recruiters will look at your résumé for less than 60 seconds—that's it!

Just like you might flip through a magazine, every day recruiters are flipping through a "magazine" of résumés. We are looking to hire someone for a job opening that we have. We have a need and want to "purchase" someone's skills for our company. If someone were flipping through a magazine and saw your ad, would they want to purchase your skills for their company? You have one document to highlight how awesome you are—your résumé is your chance to shine.

In this chapter, I break the résumé into five sections to focus on individually. I will then go over some tips and some dos and don'ts for your résumé. I will end the chapter with comments from recruiters who filled out my survey. You will see that the résumé is a hot topic for recruiters.

CONTACT INFORMATION

The very top of your résumé will show your contact information. You may think, *Duh, OK, moving on, I don't need a whole paragraph to learn about how to put my contact information on my résumé*. Well, stop right there because I guarantee, you may have it wrong on your résumé. Trust me; I've seen so many issues with the first part of the résumé that made me not want to even read on.

Your contact information should consist of your first and last name, e-mail address, mobile and home phone numbers, and address. For certain art-focused positions, I also like to see your website's URL or a link to your demo reel. Your e-mail address should be professional. If you have an e-mail address like **FineGirl24@yahoo.com** or **Mr.Swagg200@gmail. com**, I recommend changing it to just your name, followed by some numbers. Make it easy to remember and easy for me to type—and again, make it professional.

I recommend creating an e-mail account just for your job-searching activity. This will make it easy for you to track the e-mails you have received regarding your employment and will keep you more organized.

Your mobile number should have a professional voice-mail greeting. I don't want to hear your favorite song or anything else besides your lovely voice telling me to leave a message. Find yourself a quiet room and take the time to create a short, sweet, and professional voice-mail greeting.

When it comes to your home phone number, the best advice I have is to communicate to your family that potential employers may be calling. If your children answer your home phone, please teach them how to take a proper message. Nothing is worse than when I call people and their children are rude to me, hang up on me, or don't write down the message.

This may go without saying, but also tell your husband or wife that potential employers will be calling. I called someone whose wife picked up and gave me the third degree, thinking I was someone who was having an affair with her husband. She grilled me with questions and then insisted that her husband did not apply to my opening because he is happy at his current job. Wow, yes, please communicate to anyone who may be picking up the phone number you list on your résumé that potential employers may be calling.

With regard to your home address, you can simply put the city, state, and zip code on your résumé. I want to know where you are living. If you are located in California and I'm calling from Florida at 9:00 a.m. EST, that is 6:00 a.m. PST, and you are most likely asleep. I just want to make sure I call you at a proper time. Recruiters also want to know where you live to know if they would need to relocate you for their opening. It can help us find you a job that is close to you. As you see, there is a lot to the contact information on your résumé. We will now move on to the career summary.

CAREER SUMMARY

The career summary is the new "objective." Objectives are one of my biggest annoyances on résumés. I already know that your objective is to get the job you are applying for, to work your way up through the chain, and to be the best x, y, and z employee....Boring! Most of my fellow recruiters who filled out my survey agree with me.

The survey asked the recruiters the following question: "Would you rather see an objective or career summary on top of a résumé?" The results were as expected—22.8 percent want to see an objective, and 77.2 percent prefer a career summary.

In my opinion, you can't go wrong with a career summary.

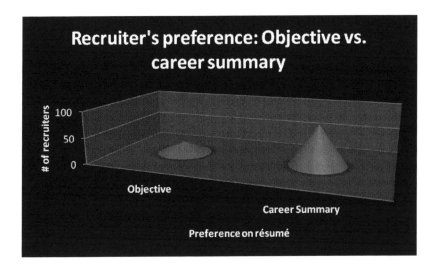

I will explain how to create the best career summary by giving you an analogy first. If you were in an elevator with the CEO of the company you wanted to work for and had only ten floors to give him a speech about why he needs to hire you for the role, what would you say? You might say, "Hello, Mr. CEO. My objective is to be a part of your team. I'm looking to enhance my skills at your corporation by providing the best customer service to your clients. I'm looking for a managerial role at your company."

Do you think Mr. CEO would want to hire you from that elevator speech? I don't think so.

Instead, you should say something like this: "Hello, Mr. CEO. I'm an established customer service manager with more than eight years of experience. I excel at developing state-of-the-art data-management tools to enhance a company's customer resource management software. I have a proven record of exceeding my clients' expectations and have high expectations for any team I work on. I achieve great results when I work in a team setting with strict deadlines and goals to achieve."

Now, do you think Mr. CEO would like to learn more about you? I'm confident that he would call his recruiter to set up an interview.

Now, treat your résumé like that. Your career summary is your elevator pitch. You have only sixty seconds to grab a recruiter's attention, so your career summary needs to summarize what you can do for the company, period.

The career summary should be five to eight sentences long, and it needs to highlight all your achievements and very clearly convey who you are as a professional. It should also be tailored to the role you are applying for. If the role you are applying for requires a lot of project management, then you need to highlight your project management experience in the career summary. Your career summary should grab the attention of the recruiter or hiring manager, so please spend time in developing the best career summary you can.

Below are some samples of some awesome career summaries to help you get the ball rolling.

CAREER SUMMARY SAMPLE 1 (MARKETING PROFESSIONAL)

Tenured eCommerce Marketing and Business Development Professional with proven results in increasing company brand recognition and exposure on the Internet, raising revenue, and managing large teams effectively. Possesses superior search engine optimization (SEO) skills to achieve first page and, in most cases, first position within organic listings on all popular search engines for targeted keywords; search engine marketing (SEM); Pay

Per Click (PPC) marketing; online retail marketing; and affiliate marketing. Demonstrated superior management with all marketing and sales efforts.

CAREER SUMMARY SAMPLE 2 (SALES MANAGEMENT PROFESSIONAL)

Experienced at managing small and large internal sales teams. More than fifteen years' experience training, mentoring, coaching, and motivating sales professionals. Established track record of managing top performing teams and recognized for numerous team sales awards. Known for ability to solve complex sales challenges, team moral, and team chemistry issues.

CAREER SUMMARY SAMPLE 3 (CUSTOMER SERVICE PROFESSIONAL)

A natural leader with a passion for mentoring and assisting other team members. Able to both give and take direction well. Customer service professional with experience working within banking, collections, finance, and the mortgage industry. Works extremely well with team members and thrives to achieve high levels of customer satisfaction.

CAREER SUMMARY SAMPLE 4 (TECHNOLOGY MANAGER PROFESSIONAL)

Senior technology manager with almost twenty years of information technology and software development experience. Broad, hands-on managerial expertise in full life-cycle enterprise-level software development, large-scale systems integration projects, and mission-critical website architecture including implementation, operations, performance engineering, and hosting. Excellent communication and interpersonal skills from both technical and business perspectives.

CAREER SUMMARY SAMPLE 5 (ADMINISTRATIVE ASSISTANT PROFESSIONAL)

Dynamic and self-directed professional with extensive experience in organizational administration, computer/technical support, and office management. Exceptional administrative assistant with superior organizational skills; effective in the management of top organizational initiatives. Background includes management/staff support, shipment scheduling, report development, and creation of executive-level internal and external correspondence.

EDUCATION

The next section on your résumé is the place where you should highlight your education history. You need just one or two lines that inform me of your college's name and what degree you received—that's all. Please do not put your graduation date unless you graduated within the past five years. By putting your graduation date on your résumé, you might be doing yourself an injustice because a graduation date is a way to figure out your age.

If you were on the dean's list, it is OK to include that. I often receive questions about whether or not to put a GPA in the education section. The best way to approach this is if you did not get a 3.5 or higher GPA, then do not put your GPA on your résumé; it's as simple as that.

If you have no formal college education or went to college but dropped out, then simply put your high school information and graduation date. If you have completed a college degree, then there is no need to put where and when you graduated from high school. I'm aware that if you have a college degree, then you received your high school diploma.

If you are currently enrolled in college, then please put where you are going to school, what you are majoring and minoring in, and your expected graduation date. Please do not list what courses you are taking that are relevant to the position you are applying to. Learning something from a book is different from actually doing it in the real world. In chapter 13, I discuss advice for college students and new graduates.

Here is a great sample of how your educational summary should look on your résumé—short and straight to the point.

E D U C A T I O N

Master's Certificate in Project Management, George Washington University

Bachelor of Arts in Psychology, University of Central Florida

Associate of Arts, Valencia Community College, dean's list

If you are currently enrolled:

E D U C A T I O N

Bachelor of Arts in Psychology, University of Central Florida, expected graduation spring 2015

Instead of abbreviating a Bachelor of Arts degree as a BA degree and a Bachelor of Science degree as BS, take the time to spell out what the degree is specifically. I do not want to guess what these letters mean.

P R O F E S S I O N A L   E X P E R I E N C E

The professional experience section is the meat and potatoes of your résumé. It will hold the most substance, and is your opportunity to shine. This section of your résumé highlights your best accomplishments at each of your places of employment, and tells me what you can do for my company.

A great way to start the professional experience section is to write a list of all the companies you worked for in chronological order for the past fifteen years—if you have that many years of experience; if not, just list what you can—with the most recent employment at the top.

Next, create a list of five achievements under each company.

The best way to figure out what you achieved is to answer these questions: Did you receive any awards or special recognitions? Did you create a new process or policy? Were you promoted quickly? Were you managing a team that achieved some positive results? Did you meet and exceed any of your goals? Were you responsible for any new innovations? Did you help reduce any costs for your company? Were you directly responsible for bringing in money or generating new business? Did you turn around a team's morale or work environment? Did you fix anything or solve any problems? These accomplishments will show your value and what you achieved for each company.

The professional experience is *not* the job description. I read numerous résumés in which candidates have simply copied and pasted their previous positions' job descriptions as their professional experience. *I do not want to see a list of your responsibilities*; that does not tell me anything about what you can do for my company. I want to see what you accomplished while you were there and what you achieved that was special, making you a superstar candidate.

Here is an example of what your list should look like:

2008–Present: Top Talent, LLC, Customer Service Manager

- Was promoted to management within six months of employment
- Created and implemented a new reporting structure
- Trained employees, resulting in the team leading for performance in the state.
- Won the Top Customer Service Manager Award in the region eight times in three years.
- Consistently received a 100 percent customer-satisfaction rating on team's survey results.

2003–2008: Recruiting Enterprises, Customer Service Associate

- Completed a two-year training program in one year.

- Was promoted from an intern to customer service associate after three years of service.
- Won the Top Customer Service Associate Award.
- Created new hire training program.
- Had the best conversion rate of cold calls to sales.

Once you have created a list of all of your employment history and achievements for the companies you have worked for, you need to go back and fill in more details. Recruiters like to see numbers and specifics. If you were on a team, we want to know how many were on that team. If you won an award, explain what that award means. Be specific; pretend that I do not know anything about your role and achievements. I need you to spell it out exactly.

I've added in bold what you should now add to the list below.

2008–Present: Top Talent, LLC, Customer Service Manager

- **Received the only promotion out of twenty-three associates** from **customer service associate** to **customer service manager** within six months of employment.
- **Independently** created and implemented a new reporting structure **that reached more than one hundred locations and saved Top Talent, LLC, $5,000 in reporting services.**
- Trained **twenty-two customer service reps in a seven-month period,** which resulted in the team **receiving the status of the number-one team in the district for six months in a row among thirty-four teams** in **Florida.**
- **Received** the Top Customer Service Manager Award eight **times** in three years **among thirty-four managers in the region.**
- **Responsible for leading a team that received a 100 percent customer-satisfaction rating three years straight on the team's survey, which resulted in national recognition and the team being awarded a satisfaction plaque.**

2003–2008: Recruiting Enterprises—Customer Service Associate

- **Became the first person to** complete a training program in one year that was designed to be completed in two years. **Received regional recognition for the work completed in the training program.**

- Promoted over **fifteen other interns** from **customer service administrator** to customer service associate after three years of service.
- **Received the highly prestigious Outstanding Customer Service Award six times in five years of employment.**
- Created new hire training program **which was adopted corporate-wide**.
- **Consistently produced a high conversion rate (45 percent) of cold calls resulting in sales.**

After reviewing the samples above, do you see the amount of specific information that is needed? I need to know what you did and what resulted. The main point to remember is to be specific. Now that you have highlighted your accomplishments and spelled out more specifics on those achievements, you are ready to move on to the skills section of your résumé.

SKILLS

The skills section is meant mostly for technical skills. Please do not list skills like sales, communication, people skills, negotiating, being a team player, being proactive, and so on. Listing those items does not tell me anything. If you have those skills, I will assume a lot of that based on your experience and accomplishments. Again, the skills section is for technical skills. Here is where you will list any software programs in which you are proficient or have working knowledge. Please do not list a program you have not used in many years and barely knew how to use then. If you put it on your résumé, we assume you know how to use the program and may ask you to perform certain functions in the software program.

Below are some examples of a good skills section of a résumé. As you can see, it's simply a list—there's no need for any other information. You may not have as many technical skills on your résumé as are shown in the examples below, but that is completely OK. Just listing the Microsoft programs you are familiar with will work. Notice that the title and the presentation of the skills are formatted differently in each example; I do not care what you label it or how you format it.

SOFTWARE:

Crystal/Ad Hoc and Cube Reports; CampusVue; Engrade; Moodle; TaskStream; Blackboard; Learning Management System; EmployFlorida.com; Florida Ready to Work; A+; Apex; SIS; ePEP; World Client; TERMS; Open Office; Microsoft: Outlook, Word, Publisher, PowerPoint, Excel, Visio, Project, Access; knowledge of PeopleSoft and SharePoint

TECHNICAL TRAINING/SKILLS

Agile Software Development • IBM Rational Unified Process • Cisco Certified Network Associate (CCNA)

Rational Software Architect • Oracle SQL/ MySQL, Hibernate • J2EE Enterprise Solutions

Eclipse IDE and RCP design • XML PERL, PHP, JSP • UNIX WebLogic, Apache

SKILLS:

Apple Certified Final Cut Pro Professional Level One, Final Cut 7, Final Cut X, Motion; Adobe Premier, Encore, Photoshop, and Audition; Microsoft Office: Word, Excel, and PowerPoint.

I hope I've helped you get the ball rolling with writing your résumé or making corrections on your current résumé. As mentioned in the beginning of this chapter, your résumé is your advertisement. You have only sixty seconds or less to grab a recruiter's attention, so please take the time to create the best résumé possible.

If you are still having issues, there are numerous professional writing agencies and professional writers you can hire to create your résumé for you. They may be pricey, but take it from me: They are worth it.

Below are some do's and don'ts for résumé writing.

D O :

- Go from general to very specific statements.
- Remember to customize your résumé to cater to each position you are applying for.
- Keep the font and page layout easy to follow and read.
- Include a career summary.
- Keep your résumé updated; this is a living document to which you should always be adding.
- Seek professional résumé-writing help if you need to; it is well worth it.
- Make sure your jobs are in chronological order, with the most recent at the top.

D O N ' T :

- Write your résumé in first person. Nowhere on your résumé should I see "I," "me," or "we."
- Have any grammatical or spelling errors on your résumé.
- Include your Social Security number or any personal information other than the contact information described in this chapter.
- Use a bunch of fluff or keywords with little substance.
- Include a picture of yourself on your résumé unless you are auditioning for a movie or a modeling position.
- Lie.
- Forget to put dates.
- Include an objective.
- Copy a job description and paste it on your résumé.
- Put "References upon request" at the end of your résumé. I know you will provide references if I ask; there is no need to put that on your résumé.
- "Guess" the dates of your past employment; go through your files if you need to find a month and year you worked.
- Include extracurricular activities or hobbies (unless they relate specifically to the job you are interested in). I don't care about any of that. I just want to know what value you can bring to my company.

Finally, here is an unedited list of comments from actual recruiters who participated in my survey. At this point, none of this should be a surprise to you.

RÉSUMÉ ADVICE FROM RECRUITERS WHO COMPLETED THE SURVEY

- "Each job is different, so be sure your résumé matches each one specifically. Yes, its more work, but it will yield better results."
- "Repost your résumé every few days on career sites. Make your résumé 'easy on the eyes,' not too long, and use bullet points to describe your responsibilities."
- "Volunteer to show that you are doing something other than sitting at home. Put that experience on your résumé. Get LinkedIn."
- "Résumé format catches eyes. Always sound humble and thankful."
- "Keep your résumé updated."
- "Get professional résumé help."
- "Making it easy for an employer to see how your skills and experience match with the position you are applying for will get you a much quicker response. Don't be general on your résumé and cover letter. Submit a cover letter with your application, even if it is just a short paragraph."
- "Make sure your résumé reflects some if not all the experience or knowledge the job posting or job you are applying for requires."
- "Keep résumé to two pages max, only put relevant information, and tailor your résumé to the job."

THINGS THAT APPLICANTS DO ON THEIR RÉSUMÉ THAT BOTHER RECRUITERS

- "Résumés that are not up-to-date."
- "Résumés in the first person!"
- "Being wishy-washy…not being clear on their résumé, over exaggerating their experience, not being committed to the job search and interview process."

- "Spelling mistakes on a résumé. Unprepared for the interview. Not researching the company."
- "Copying and pasting the job description for the job they worked, and putting it in their résumé without putting it in their own words."
- "When they don't change their résumé/cover letter and send it to my company stating they want to work at another!!! Misspelled words. When they forget to include their e-mail address on their résumé! That is my main way of communicating vs. phone. And make sure it is a professional e-mail address vs. a 'funny' one."
- "Lying via résumé or interview."
- "Poorly written résumés and a lack of desire to heed helpful advice from recruiting managers prior to interviews."
- "Grammar or spelling mistakes as well as unprofessional e-mails."
- "Résumés all about nothing, or buzz-word bingo. Make sure to only list skills you are an expert in and have been involved in personally. No one cares if your 'company' uses certain technology. The bigger question is: Did you build it or design it?"

CHAPTER 8

TWENTY APPLICATIONS A DAY, NO CALLBACKS—WHAT GIVES?

"Every day is a NEW day. You will survive. And we can hear and smell desperation."

ANONYMOUS, CORPORATE RECRUITER

While looking for employment, the application process can be one of the most difficult, painstaking stages. Get ready to work hard and then wait. Get ready to be rejected, turned down, and disappointed. Prepare yourself to put in long hours and to be patient. In today's economy, getting your "dream" job is like winning the lottery. There are more applicants out there than open jobs. You may be competing with hundreds or thousands of others for one job. My goal is to give you an arsenal of information to help your odds increase drastically. Let's dive in.

First, you need to do these things: Formulate a clear idea of what companies you would like to work for, have a selected career goal in mind, make sure your résumé is up-to-date and cleaned up, have a professional e-mail address, change your voice-mail message to be professional, make sure all of your social-media sites are private, and communicate to members of your household that they should expect to receive phone calls from possible employers. Now you are ready to apply for the jobs you are interested in.

Do not just sit down one day and randomly start applying to everything you see on the Internet. Slow down until you have completed everything I mentioned above.

If you are unemployed, your new job is to find employment. You will wake up every morning as if you were going to work. Conduct your normal routine like your morning exercise, showering, getting dressed, eating breakfast, and having a cup of coffee. Then by 9:00 a.m., sit down and get online.

You will remain on the computer or phone until lunchtime. You will have an hour lunch break and then get back to the computer. Then around 4:30 p.m., you will write down the companies you want to contact and things to follow up on the next day. You will continue this basic routine Monday through Friday until guess when? Do you think you will do this until you are tired? Until you get impatient? Until you have better plans during the day? Nope, you will continue this routine daily until you have an offer letter in your hand ready to sign.

On the first day, I want you to set aside three hours to set up your basic free LinkedIn (LI) profile. If you already have a LinkedIn profile, skim through this section. You will pick up some tips for optimizing your profile. I don't care how old you are, or how much experience you have or don't have, and I don't care if you hate social media. I'm standing firm by saying that if you are looking for a job, then you *must* get on LinkedIn.

Recruiters like me are on LinkedIn daily, looking for top talent for our roles. If you don't have a profile, I won't be able to find you, period. Having a LI profile allows you to stay in *professional contact* with all of your previous coworkers, and connects you with large groups of professional people. It's not like Facebook, which is very personal; LI is for professional use only. LinkedIn allows you to go beyond just posting on a job board; it allows you to communicate with people in your industry, or in industries you want to enter.

So you may be asking yourself, *what is a LinkedIn profile, and what do I put on it?*

LI profiles are basically your résumé in a simplistic format. You put in your profile what is on your résumé. When you create your profile, LI will walk you through the process step-by-step, which includes uploading your résumé. Don't worry; you can remove your address from any documents you want. LinkedIn also will ask you to upload a picture. This goes without saying, but your profile picture should be a nice, polished head shot. This is not the same as your Facebook or other pictures. The LinkedIn picture should be professional.

Once you have created your profile, you now need to grow your network. Your network is anyone you know through your professional or personal life. You want a large network because the larger your network, the more visibility you will have for recruiters to see you and the more visibility you will have to companies. You can communicate only with people who are connected with you. For others to communicate with you or view your entire profile, they must ask you to connect with them. The goal is to get as many connections as you can.

Here is how a network works. Let's say you worked with Tina Sans, so you request Tina Sans to connect with you. She accepts. Now you have full access to all of Tina Sans's contacts. Let's say Tina knows someone who works for the company you are hoping to work for. You can e-mail Tina and ask her to make an introduction. Just like that, you have a connection within the company you want to work for; it's that easy.

Below is a step-by-step strategy for growing your network on LinkedIn.

1. Start with past coworkers, search for your old company, and search their employees; you will find people you know.
2. Search for the schools you attended and link up with fellow alumni from each school.
3. Have LI automatically search your Twitter, e-mail, Facebook, and Pinterest accounts, and other contacts, and those sites will immediately connect you on LI with all those people. BOOM! Immediate networks!

4. Search for your friends and family members.
5. Search LI groups to connect immediately to other people who are in the industry you want to be in, and send a request to be a part of the group.

By following these four steps, you should be able to grow your network quickly in a few days. Keep in mind that you get a maximum of one hundred profile searches per month, so you cannot sit down and search for random people all day. Your searches are limited to prevent people from connecting to or harassing people they do not know.

Once you have built your network, feel free to start to message people and let them know you are looking for employment. Be specific about what you want and ask for it. Message previous coworkers to let them know you are in the market, and ask them to connect you with people they may know who are hiring. You will be amazed at what LinkedIn will do for you while you are looking for a job.

Once you have completed setting up your LinkedIn profile and are actively reaching out to your network, start to make some phone calls to people you already know. If you want the help of an employment agency or headhunter, take the time to research the best agency for you and give them a call. They will conduct an interview with you, help you with your résumé, possibly set up an in-person interview with one or more companies, and help you line up some interviews. It cannot hurt to seek the professional expertise of these agencies. The main thing to keep in mind is that they are resources for you; you still need to continue your efforts as well.

Now you are ready to apply to some openings.

During the application stage, you will be applying for jobs on companies' websites. As a recruiter, I post my openings on two different sites: my company's website and LinkedIn. Other recruiters may post on many other career sites like hotjob.com, monster.com, and careerbuilder.com.

The website www.indeed.com is a search engine that will search the entire Internet and find jobs that match your request. Indeed saves you time because you don't need to search a lot of sites; it combines them all into one site.

Here is a big tip. Are you listening? As you apply to openings on the Internet, create a spreadsheet or Word document listing the following items: the date you applied, the name of the company you applied to, and the job title you applied for. Also make a note about why you applied to the position and what interested you in the company. This list will come in handy once you start to receive callbacks from recruiters; trust me.

Secondly, if an online application asks you to fill in your work history, *do not* type in that field "See résumé." If you do that, *you will automatically get declined*.

Putting "See résumé" there shows that you are incredibly lazy. It also shows that you do not care enough to take the time to fill in that section of the application. So you may ask, *Why do I have to fill out all that information when it is all on my résumé?*

Here is why: An application is a legal document. What you put on it must be true and is legally binding. A résumé is not a legal document. So while you may be required to attach a résumé, you are also required to fill out an application because it is a legal document. If you end up getting an on-site interview, you may be asked to complete an application again. *Do not* staple your résumé to the application and say, "See résumé." That is a great way to upset a recruiter and not be considered for the job.

Corporate recruiters and agency recruiters normally work on Applicant Tracking Systems or ATSs. The ATS is a database that filters applications of those people who apply to the recruiters' specific openings, which are called "requisitions" or "REQs." Here is the big secret: Most ATSs allow recruiters to set up filters to automatically *disqualify* someone if they do not meet a certain requirement.

So guess what that means? If you do not meet the minimum requirements for the job I posted, I won't even see your résumé; you will be turned down automatically.

This is why I mentioned in chapter 5 to stop applying to openings for which you do not meet the minimum qualifications; you are wasting your time. An example of a filter I may set up is one for years of experience or education. If you do not meet a certain experience level or education, then I will not see your application. You will also not be considered or will not have your application viewed by a recruiter if you filled out the application incorrectly. Some filters are set up to automatically disqualify someone who doesn't take the time to complete the application, so please keep that in mind. Slow things down and take the time to follow the entire application process.

Applicant Tracking Systems also have the ability to send out automatic e-mails when the recruiter changes the status of your application.

So, if I decide to pursue other candidates, you may get a turn-down e-mail. When you receive these e-mails they are sent from a system, and it means the recruiter moved you in the process one way or the other.

Finally, as I screen through the résumés that are funneled into my requisitions, for each résumé I view, I must state a reason why I did not consider that applicant for the position. This is called "disqualifying a candidate."

Applicant Tracking Systems usually have a lot of options from which a recruiter can choose. The disqualifying options to choose from might include "not considered due to location," "salary requirements too high," "skills are not a fit," "immigration issues," "unable to reach candidate," "candidate doesn't meet minimum requirements," "education," "employment history," "candidate no longer interested," "candidate no longer available," "candidate withdrew from process," "ineligible background check," "misrepresentation," or "relocation not available." So as you apply to the position, ask yourself if any of these disqualifying factors relate to you.

If so, don't waste your time.

Once you have spent a week or so building your LinkedIn network and have spent some time on the Internet applying to everything you are interested in and qualified for, you are now ready to get your networking game on.

In the survey conducted of the 101 recruiters in the United States, I asked the following question: "Please state where most of your hires come from."

More than 70 percent of the responses indicated that hires were from the recruiters' own network and referrals. The rest were from their company website, LinkedIn, and career boards like monster.com and careerbuilder.com.

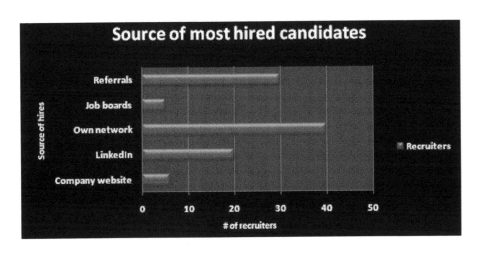

So what does this mean to you? This means you have a 70 percent higher chance of getting a job by networking with people who work at the company where you want to work and with recruiters than by applying to jobs you find on the Internet.

I've spoken to many unemployed people who say, "I send out hundreds of applications a week, and I never hear anything back. I feel like I just keep throwing my résumé into a black hole."

Well, my follow-up question to them is, "Are you networking outside of the Internet? Have you talked to your friends and family to see who they know?" Most of the time, the answer is no.

Your next assignment is to plan to get out and network at least two times per week. This does not mean talking on the phone; it means getting out of your house and meeting people face-to-face.

By creating your LinkedIn profile, you have already established a great way to network. If you have joined some networking groups on LI, make sure you reach out to people who are working where you want to work or who currently work in the job you want. Ask to shadow them. Ask them to meet you for coffee or lunch. Reach out to them to see if they would be open to speaking to you about how they got where they are now. People love to talk about their own success. I receive calls from aspiring recruiters regularly, and I rarely turn down an opportunity to meet people for coffee to help them achieve their goals. Most professionals are open to helping in the same way, so just ask.

Finally, research local networking groups in your area and attend their events. This is a great way to meet local professionals. Even if the people who are in these groups do not do exactly what you want to do, you are networking; they may know someone to whom they can introduce you. It's that easy. This is a huge part of the job application stage.

Not only must you sit in front of the computer, you must get yourself out into the world and meet people.

At the end of the survey, I asked the recruiters to tell me some secrets to share with job hunters. I've added the comments that related to networking here. Now you know I'm not making this stuff up; these are comments from real recruiters across the country.

- "Networking is key."
- "Network, network, network. Simply responding to a job posting is not enough. Find someone in the company and network with them."
- "Network with everyone. Use LinkedIn and personal networks and professional groups."
- "Network, network, network. Then do some more networking."
- "Get out there and find something that you like, and work hard at making it work for you."
- "Be proactive and network...utilize social networking. Don't rely on job boards...don't just apply/submit a résumé and pray."
- "Make finding a job a full-time job."
- "Don't be afraid to use your network or to reach out to a recruiter directly. It shows initiative."
- "Network and keep your skills sharp."
- "Hit the pavement and network/stay active in job search. When you do find a position, stick around/show loyalty as opposed to jumping ship frequently."
- "Be positive; no matter how discouraged you are, do not share that with potential employers."
- "There are plenty of jobs. You need to ask yourself, do you want to be not working at $80k a year, or do you want to be working at $45k with full benefits? Not that I'm suggesting that people need to take that kind of cut in pay, but this thought process helps people face the realities of the marketplace and possibly open avenues they might not have considered."
- "A good portion of people gain employment by who they know. If you don't have connections, take the time to research and tailor both résumé and cover letter to target companies."
- "Always follow the application process; don't try to find ways around it. Don't have errors on your résumé. Don't apply to my job opening if your résumé does not contain any of the requirements stated in a position posting."
- "Please, don't 'interview by texting' with a series of online questions rather than taking the time and writing a decent e-mail

message highlighting your qualifications and expressing your interest."

- "Don't let the job hunt bring you down. Stay positive and keep putting your best foot forward. Being employed is better than not getting a paycheck, so don't be afraid to take a job that you may feel overqualified for. You can always continue to interview to find that awesome job you have been waiting for."

You are now in the longest stage of attaining employment. The application stage is very tedious and requires a lot of patience and persistence. Keep up the daily routine and treat finding a job like a full-time job. Keep your LinkedIn profile active, continue to find contacts, apply to openings you are interested in *and* qualified for, and finally, get out of the house two times a week to meet with people and network.

During the application stage, stay positive, energetic, focused, and organized. Goods things will come from this dedication. I guarantee you, 90 percent of the applicants out there will not do this— until they read this book, of course.

Below is more advice from the survey I conducted with the recruiters. These are comments directly from current recruiters on how to approach the application stage.

- "Don't have a negative attitude when looking for work. When I talk to people and they tell me how it is so hard out there, how they are not getting hired because of their age, etc.—this is a major turn-off! Always have a positive attitude when speaking with recruiters."
- "Acting desperate is a big, red flag. You have to convey that you want the job you are applying for, not just any job."
- "Ensure the résumé meets the requirements of the job you are seeking."
- "Have a game plan and follow up on all résumé submittals to show your eagerness to join their team."
- "Target the companies and industries you are passionate about; 80 percent of the interview is personality fit."
- "Don't give up. Don't be late for interviews. Dress appropriately for interviews. *Never put 'see résumé' on an application*. If you

can't fill out an application as we ask, then that's the first sign that you have trouble following directions. It may be a pain, but the application is our *legal* document, and your résumé is not."

- "Don't make it sound like you are looking for a job when a lot of the time you are only wasting time."
- "Don't give up, be persistent in your search, and make sure your résumé speaks to the position you are applying for."
- "Take any job. Some money is better than no money."

CHAPTER 9

CONGRATULATIONS—YOU HAVE A PHONE INTERVIEW!

"You will never believe this; I called a candidate today for our scheduled phone interview, and she had a talk show on in the background. I can tell you after our call, I now know that two men are not the father and one is the father. Needless to say, I will not be calling her again."

SHAWNNA ADAMSON, UNIVERSITY RELATIONS MANAGER

Once you receive a phone call from a recruiter, you have now entered the interview process. You are formally a candidate for the position. This means the recruiter liked what he or she saw on your résumé, and you met the minimum qualifications for the position.

The first phone conversation is meant to cover some major things. The conversation is going to uncover your personality, your communication abilities, your professionalism, your skills in greater detail, and show overall if you are a candidate the recruiter would want to put his or her reputation on the line for and send to the hiring manager.

What most people are not aware of is that at the time of the phone interview, recruiters are making the decision to either represent you as your "agent" or move on. If I decide to take you on as a "client," that means I'm confident in you and your abilities and feel you are worth my hiring manager's precious time. So in that call, you must impress me; otherwise, I'm not going to send you to the hiring manager for an interview—that's it.

The way to impress a recruiter is to be very uncomplicated, friendly, and positive. I don't care if the weather is horrible or you just got a flat tire and are sitting on the side of the road. I want to hear that you are having a great day and are happy I called. I need to hear enthusiasm and excitement in your voice. You have only ten seconds to make a first impression, so over the phone you should be overly personable.

I understand that sometimes I might catch you off-guard or in the middle of something; however, if you are interested in working at my company, you will need to put your personal stresses aside for my phone call. If I've called at truly the wrong time, simply ask if there is a better time when we can connect so that you will not have any distractions. I will not mind you showing that you value the call and want to be 100 percent focused on the conversation and not preoccupied, so that is completely acceptable. Then, when I do call you, please make sure there aren't any distractions in the background. I don't want to hear traffic in the background, children crying, people talking, the TV, or the radio. All I want to hear is your lovely voice.

Just as much as those things are diverting your attention on the other end of the phone, they are equally as distracting to me and show me you have not taken the time to plan out a simple thirty minutes to an hour of focused, uninterrupted time to discuss your possible future career.

I would like to now remind you of the tip I stated in chapter 8. As you apply to openings on the Internet, create a spreadsheet or Word document listing the following items: the date you applied, the name of the company you applied to, and the job title you applied for. Also make a note regarding why you applied to the position and what interested you in the company.

When a recruiter calls you, you want to be familiar with the job you applied for and with the company. So keeping a log of everything you are applying for will help you when you receive a phone call. I can honestly say I get extremely annoyed when I call someone and this is their response: "I'm sorry. I've applied to so many jobs; I can't remember which one this is. Can you please remind me?"

That right there will immediately turn me off because if you applied to my opening, you should immediately know which job you have applied for. I don't care if you applied to a hundred positions in a week; please keep a log of them. This way, if I call you, you will be able to pull up that information quickly.

Now, let's say you made it past the introduction. You have a great attitude, and you are familiar with who I am and the role you applied for. The next thing to be prepared for is to walk me through your résumé. When a recruiter says, "Tell me about your experience" or "Can you please walk me through your résumé?" here is the format you should follow and the questions you should answer as you "walk" a recruiter through your résumé.

Start from the earliest position on your résumé and move on up to your most recent role. For each role, you should tell the recruiter the following:

1. How did you find that job?
2. What you were responsible for while at that position?
3. What key accomplishment did you achieve while you were there?
4. Why did you leave?

This part of the phone interview should take about ten minutes. Carefully walk through each position and answer those four questions. After you arrive at your most recent role, please be ready to discuss why you are looking for another opportunity—without trash-talking your current employer.

As soon as you have completed walking the recruiter through your résumé, she most likely will have a lot of follow-up questions. Get ready to talk about your career goals and why you applied to the role you are interviewing for. The call should be pretty easy with regards to the questions you will be required to answer.

Remember, the main objective from this call is to get a callback or an on-site interview.

Again, the conversation is going to uncover your personality, your communication abilities, your professionalism, and your skills in greater detail. It will allow the recruiter to see, overall, if you are a candidate she would want to put her reputation on the line for. So remain friendly and comfortable to speak to throughout the entire conversation.

The recruiter will end the conversation by asking you if you have any further questions about the opportunity or the company. This is your time to ask any questions that did not get answered on the call.

Do not ask the recruiter, "Can you tell me what I would be doing?" You read the job description, so this question will make you look like you did not do your research. It is OK to ask what the next steps are. You also can ask how long the recruiter anticipates it will take to fill this role. Feel free to ask any specific questions about the team you will be working on or the manager you may be working for. It is a good idea to know the culture of the company, so use this time to ask what type of culture they have. If a recruiter does not mention salary, then please do not ask at this time what the position pays.

Every recruiter is different—some discuss salary on the very first call, and others do not. Personally, I discuss it within the first conversation. I do this because I hate wasting my time and my candidate's time. I like to set expectations from the very beginning. I'm amazed at how many recruiters wait until the candidate conducts hours of interviews and the manager is very excited to extend an offer, and then when the offer is extended, the candidate expects a lot more and ends up declining the offer. Do not become one of these candidates.

If you have not discussed salary by the time you have had one or two hours of phone or in-person interviews, then pick up the phone and call the recruiter. Let her know you are excited about the opportunity and still interested; however, before you spend any more of your time interviewing, you would like to discuss the salary for the position. Take it into your own hands to bring the topic up for discussion.

The phone interview is your one chance to make a good first impression, which hopefully will lead to an on-site interview. You must be prepared for the call and able to put your personal life aside for a moment. The call will be short but packed with a lot of information. Make sure you are ready to "walk" the recruiter through your résumé, be easy to speak to, have a positive attitude, and ask relevant questions.

Feel free to follow up with a thank-you e-mail to the recruiter and let her know you are looking forward to the next steps.

If you follow the tips in this chapter, you should feel really good about your phone interview, and substantially increase your opportunity to receive positive results.

CHAPTER 10

HOW TO BE A STAR INTERVIEWEE

"Interviewing Suzy was like trying to pull teeth. I had to probe her to answer my question completely. I thought she would have gotten the point on how to answer my questions in a complete fashion, but she didn't. I was so exhausted, I ended the interview early."

ANONYMOUS, HIRING MANAGER

As we move on in the wonderful world of getting a job, we now have entered the dreaded on-site or face-to-face interview.

At this point of the interview game you have marketed yourself on your résumé, gained the attention of a recruiter, spoken to a recruiter and possibly a hiring manager, and have now received the official news that more people at the company want to meet you. This is so exciting! I want to provide you with some secrets on interviewing that will make you more confident in your interview. My goal is for you to walk into the interview with extreme confidence and excitement. Here we go.

You may think, *Great! I have the interview. I'll get in the car on that day, put the address in my GPS, get there early, sit in the car to go over some things, and walk on in*. Hold on one second!

Prior to getting in the car, please do a drive-by to know exactly where the interview is taking place. Make sure your clothes have been cleaned and pressed the night before. The last thing you want to do is rush on the day of your interview.

On the day of your interview, have your résumé, notebook paper, and pen ready to grab easily. Be 100 percent dressed and ready for the interview. Make sure your hair and makeup is how you want it. Feel free to pop in a mint or some gum while you are on the drive, but please spit it out prior to entering the parking lot. *Do not* smoke a cigarette on your way to the interview. I know this may be hard, but nothing is more unappealing than a candidate who walks into my office reeking of cigarette smoke.

On the flip side, do not spray a bunch of cologne or perfume on, either; remember, you may be interviewing in a small office, so the smell may be abrasive to others. Ladies, do not carry a large purse into your interview. Have your keys in your pocket, and that's it. It is frustrating when a woman comes in for an interview with a huge purse, and she has to find a seat for it as if it were a person—not professional.

I know you have heard it before, but you have only one first impression, and that first impression can set the tone for the rest of your interview. From the moment you pull into the parking lot of the company, I want you to pretend that they have a video camera on you and your hiring manger is watching you.

This may sound silly; however, in one of my previous roles, my hiring manager had a window that faced the visitor parking spots for the company. He had numerous stories of candidates who would sit in their cars talking on their cell phones, fixing their hair or makeup, swishing mouthwash and spitting it out the window, smoking cigarettes, and even talking to themselves. He also saw a candidate who brought his wife and two kids with him; he watched as the guy yelled at his kids about their behavior and lost his temper with his wife. This manager formed a first impression before these candidates even knew anyone was looking.

This has also happened at other companies, where employees would see candidates doing very strange things in the parking lot and report it back to the hiring manager or myself. Keep in mind that even before your interview starts, you are on display. There's usually a security guard, receptionist, clients, or current employees with whom you will come in contact, and if you don't make a good impression on them, they may report this back to the hiring manager.

The second recommendation I know you have heard before, but still applies, is to have a firm handshake. You would be amazed at the people I interview who have the limp-noodle handshake. You can tell a lot of information about a person based on his or her handshake. A handshake immediately tells me if you are a confident person. It tells me if you are going to be proactive or reactive, it tells me if you are happy or sad, and it tells me if you are nervous or excited. When you shake someone's hand, you are making eye contact with that person as well. Eye contact also tells me a lot about who you are.

Here is another message for the ladies: The next time I get a female giving me the princess handshake, I'm going to tell her to turn around, grow some confidence, and then apply again. Seriously! Do you know what the princess handshake is? It's the handshake where she places her four fingers in my hand so lightly as if I'm supposed to kiss the top of her hand. I don't care if you are interviewing or out to dinner with friends. Stop shaking people's hands like you are a delicate princess. No, you are a professional woman looking for a job. Demand attention, demand respect, and demand that a man shake your hand like an equal human being.

When I shake a hand of a female who gives me that handshake, I immediately feel bad for her because I know she is not confident in herself. When I shake someone's hand, I want to be just as strong as or even stronger than the other person is. Practice it. Have a friend or relative shake your hand and see who can squeeze the hardest. Make it a quick squeeze, an easy shake, and include eye contact. Practice it with some other individuals and make sure you continue to shake hands in a confident way, not just when you are interviewing.

Once you make it through the parking lot, past the receptionist, and shake the hand of the recruiter or manager, you are now ready to become an interviewing STAR. That's right—for the rest of your interview; you are going to answer each question using the STAR method.

These next few paragraphs are extremely important for your inter-viewing success. I recommend highlighting these paragraphs and becom-ing an expert in the following information.

The first secret about interviewing is that companies use behavior-based interviewing questions. It's proven that your past performance is the best way to gauge what your future performance will be. With this said the majority of the interview questions are going to require you to provide examples from your past experiences.

The questions will most likely start with something like this: "Give me an example of when you…" or "Tell me about a time when you…." These are behavior-based interview questions; they are asking you to provide an example of a time when you completed a certain task. They are *not* saying, "Tell me what you *would* do." No, they are saying, "Tell me what you *have* done…." Do you see the difference? If someone asks me to tell them what I *would* do in a certain situation, I know I can make up anything and tell them what they want to hear. When someone asks me what I *have* done in the past, I must immediately think of an example and tell them what I did. It's hard to make up a story or tell them what I think they want to hear.

Now that you know what the format of the questions will be, get prepared. Begin by looking at the job description of the position you are interviewing for. I've copied and pasted a sample job description below and added in the questions you should be prepared to answer. This is something companies do not want you to figure out, so here I am liter-ally telling you the questions they are going to ask you. I feel like I'm giv-ing you answers to a test.

SKILLS AND REQUIREMENTS

Outside of raw marketing experience, teamwork and communication are the most important parts of a Sr. Product Manager's day-to-day job **(Be ready to give an example of when you have worked on a team. What role did you play, how was the team communication, and what did you do to be a val-ued member of the team?)**, whether it's managing relationships within our company or negotiating with external partners and suppliers. **(Be ready to give an example of when you had to manage a difficult relationship and negotiate with external partners—what was the outcome?)** An effective Director/Sr. Product Manager must also have a strong working knowledge of this specific industry, including market breakdown, target audiences, and competition. **(Be prepared to discuss what you know about the competition, target audience, and market breakdown.)**

Key skills include:

- Teamwork—**Give an example of when you had to work on a difficult team. What role did you play?**
- Communication—**Give an example of when you had to communicate to internal and external clients.**
- Initiative—**Give an example of when you had to take initiative.**
- Team development—**Give an example of when you had to develop a team.**
- Analytical skills—**Give an example of when you had to be analytical.**
- Digital, direct to consumer experience –**Give an example of when you had to sell directly to consumers.**
- Financial experience; ability to carefully manage a budget and navigate a profit and loss statement (P&L)—**Give an example of when you had to manage a complex budget.**
- Good client-handling abilities—**Give an example of when you had to handle a difficult client.**
- Good negotiation skills—**Give an example of when you had to negotiate a difficult offer.**
- Ability to work well within a multi-disciplinary team—**Give an example of when you had to work with cross-functional teams.**
- Strong presentation skills—**Give an example of when you had to give an important presentation. What did you do to prepare?**
- Demonstrated ability to deliver innovative programs—**Give an example of when you had to deliver an innovative program or new policy.**

Additional experience we are looking for:

- Demonstrated record of success in consumer marketing—**Give an example of when you launched a successful marketing campaign.**

- Experience working on cutting-edge, leading brands that have strong consumer awareness and interest—**Give an example of when you worked with a cutting-edge product with strong consumer awareness**.
- Experience working directly and negotiating with licensors/licensees—**Give an example of when you had to negotiate between a client and a licensor.**
- Exercises a high degree of influence and ability to impact team performance of subordinates, managers, peers, outside agencies, and executive management—**Give an example of when you influenced the decisions of others.**
- Strategic leader and thinker with ability to create exciting breakthrough marketing plans—**Give an example of when you created a groundbreaking marketing plan.**

Do you see how you can take a job description and get yourself prepared with the questions they are going to ask you? Keep in mind that if it's on the job description, you must be prepared to give examples of when you accomplished that specific task.

Now that you know what types of questions they are going to ask you, you may think all you need to do is respond—easy. Keep in mind that you should be doing 80 percent of the talking in an interview. So when you respond to the questions, be prepared to be very specific and provide examples.

There is a format that is very important for you to master. The format is called the STAR method. Once you know how to respond to these interview questions, you have immediately set yourself above the competition. Here is what STAR stands for:

Situation—Describe the situation
Task or Target—What was the goal or objective?
Action—What did you do to complete this task to reach your goal?
Result—What happened as a result of your efforts?

So suppose someone asks you a behavior-based question like, "Can you give me an example of when you had to work on a difficult project while working on a team?" Here is how your responses should sound based on the STAR method:

Situation—"I was working for a company that was going through a huge growth phase. We needed a better system to track our clients. I was chosen to be a part of a ten-person team to create the new system."

Task—"Our goal was to identify a system that worked for our needs and was within our budget. We had two months to come up with the new system and have it implemented throughout the entire company."

Action—"I stepped up and became the project leader for this task. I created a project plan that included meeting dates and times, testing times, financial plans, and vendors to meet with. Then, from the project plan, I delegated different tasks to each of the members on my team. I checked in with them daily and tracked their progress. I constantly had to move things around and adjust my plan."

Result—"The team ended up identifying a new system to use. We put together a new manual to use in training the employees, and it was well received. We were successful at hitting our deadline on budget. The company still uses this system today."

Take the time to write down the answers to your questions using the STAR method. After you practice the method a few times, it will become second nature. Using the STAR technique will enable you to answer difficult questions in a professional, fascinating, and influential manner. This is a skill you must master if you plan on getting a job. Let me repeat myself—*this is a skill you must master if you plan on getting a job.*

You are fully equipped to get yourself through the application process, phone-interview process, and now the interview process. It is up to you to make sure you maintain a high level of enthusiasm throughout the entire interview. Do not lose your energy, stay smiling the entire time, sit up straight, and maintain a strong sense of confidence. I don't care if you are interviewing with the CEO—remember they selected *you* over many other applicants, so be confident in yourself.

The next tip I have for you is to send a thank-you e-mail.

In the survey I conducted, I asked recruiters the following question: "Do you like receiving handwritten thank-you notes, or is an e-mail just fine?"

Only 16 percent responded by saying, "Handwritten for sure," while 55 percent said, "E-mail is just fine," and 29 percent said, "I don't care; it doesn't affect my opinion one way or the other."

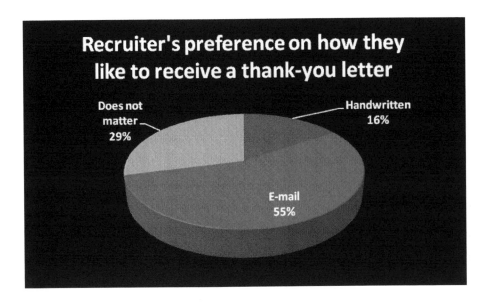

Recruiter's preference on how they like to receive a thank-you letter

Does not matter 29%

Handwritten 16%

E-mail 55%

I was actually shocked that 29 percent said they don't care either way because I definitely care. Handwritten notes are lovely, but I'm recommending *at least* sending a thank-you e-mail to the recruiter or hiring manager if you have their e-mail addresses. By sending a thank-you, you are showing your appreciation for their time, and your desire to get the job. It shows you are being courteous and that you have manners.

Please, *send a thank-you e-mail or handwritten thank-you note* after all of your in-person interviews.

Your interview should be a positive experience. Be prepared ahead of time by going over the logistics of your interview. Become familiar with possible interview questions they may ask you by looking at the job description. Get ready to answer behavior-based interview questions by providing specific examples from your past.

Finally, practice answering questions by using the STAR technique. By following the secrets and tips laid out in this chapter, you have already put yourself above the competition. Remain positive, and remember, all you are doing is talking about the best subject ever—*you!*

DOS AND DON'TS FOR INTERVIEWING

Do

- Be ten minutes early for your interview.
- Be prepared with your résumé, writing paper, and a writing utensil.
- Study the job description and come prepared with specific examples of when you have completed the job requirements in the past.
- Have a firm handshake and make eye contact.
- Be very specific in your answers, providing a lot of detail.
- Be confident and smile.
- Smile and remain positive throughout the entire interview.
- Dress according to the company culture.
- Practice the STAR technique of responding to a question.
- Send a thank-you e-mail or handwritten thank-you note.

Don't

- Be more than fifteen minutes early for your interview.
- Chew gum.
- Smoke prior to your interview.
- Take your purse or big briefcase to the interview.
- Spray on too much cologne or perfume.
- Talk about how you "would do" certain tasks; instead, talk about what you "have done" in your past.
- Talk too much or give too much personal information.
- Give general statements; the interviewer should not have to play twenty questions to get an answer out of you.
- Be arrogant or cocky.

CHAPTER 11

Secrets from Hiring Managers

"Her snobby demeanor nauseated me…seriously nauseated me."

Anonymous, hiring manager

I t may seem shocking to think that a hiring manager would say something like the quote above.

As you can see, feedback from hiring managers is always very direct and can be brutally honest at times. Keep in mind that the hiring manager has the perfect person in his or her mind for the role, and until I deliver that person, we can be pretty ruthless about what we want.

I conduct numerous meetings with my hiring managers to ensure that what they want has not changed, and to go over each candidate who is presented to them. Here's a secret: Sometimes the HMs don't really know what they want until I present a candidate. That's right; they have an image of the ideal person for the role in their mind, but they sometimes don't know their exact needs until they have the interview. So this is your time to show them that they are looking for you!

I've noticed that if you are the very first person to interview, your chances of getting the job are slim to none.

Think about it—if I send a manager one candidate to interview and let him know I have some more on the way, what do you think he will do? What would you do if you went on a blind date and knew for a fact you had five more scheduled in the next week? Do you think you would pick the very first person? Nope, you will want to see how much better the other dates will be. Your first date is your measuring stick, and you want to see how the others can be *better* than the first.

It's the same thing with recruiting. By being the first candidate, you set the bar; now all the other people after you will be looking to be better than you. If they are not, then the manager will of course circle back to you, but I'm pretty confident your chances have gone down drastically. So while persistence and being first may sound appealing, if you speak to a recruiter and he or she says you are the first to interview for the role, I would try to get your interview pushed back a week so that others can be interviewed. Then when you go in, you can demonstrate how remarkable you are and that the search can stop.

Here is another secret: You may be 100 percent qualified for the role, but if the manager does not see you clicking well with the other members of the team, then he will not hire you. Companies all have a certain "culture"—it can be laid-back, casual, corporate, creative, liberal, conservative, and so on. It is important to research the type of culture that exists in the company with which you are interviewing.

I worked in the banking industry for more than four years and had a hiring manager who would not hire anyone if the person had on a colorful suit, didn't wear a tailored suit, or had open-toed shoes on. Yes, that is right. It sounds very rigid, but that's what the banking culture was like. The people in that role were handling people's finances; they were dealing with upper-class clients, so the candidates' dress and presentation were huge factors in the hiring decision. In the interview, they had to be very prim and proper, sit up straight, and have a firm handshake. The men had to be clean-shaven, and the women had to have their hair pulled back.

On the flip side, if you are interviewing for a more creative type of industry then the attire is totally different. I've worked for a more laid back company and if someone came in wearing a suit, it made everyone feel uncomfortable. The culture was very creative; we didn't care what you look like or wear and we encouraged people to be themselves. The point is to make sure you know what type of culture the company has. Ask the recruiter if you do not know. Because your appearance is a huge deciding factor in your ability to get the job, we want to make sure you will fit in.

Keep in mind that the HM's job is not to interview or recruit; his job is to perform the responsibilities of his own job function like managing issues on his team or attending executive meetings. Also, remember that the people you are interviewing with are lacking a person on their team, so they may be taking on extra work. A hiring manager's time is extremely limited. Do not get offended if he does not spend as much time with you as you expected.

The three main questions hiring managers want answered by the end of their interviews are: "Can you do the work needed for the position and *exceed* their expectations?" and "Can you fit in with the team?" Finally, the most important question of all is, "Will you be a pain in the butt to manage?" That's it right there—that is all the HM needs to know.

No matter what position you are interviewing for, the theme is the same for what hiring managers are looking for in their interviews. They are looking for employees who will try to figure out the answer to their questions prior to seeking help. They want employees who are proactive about figuring out that there is a problem prior to it happening. They want someone who will "play well with others," someone who is on time and reliable, and someone who is ethically sound. They want people who will be easy to manage, fit in with the team, hold the ability to solve their own problems, and overall do a good job.

This goes for any role and any industry.

CHAPTER 12

The Moment You've Been Waiting For: The Offer

"My favorite part about being a recruiter is when I have a candidate accept my offer. It's pure happiness!"

Pola LoBello, senior sourcing recruiter

The offer is the highlight of my day, and also the most stressful part. This stage in the interviewing game is where things get real. This is the time when I put everything I have to offer on the table and tell you what my company feels you are worth to them. The offer is a very personal conversation between the candidate and me. As mentioned in a previous chapter, I want to hire you. Along that same line, I want to give you the maximum wage; after all, it isn't *my* money. There is a lot that goes into an offer, so I would like to help you understand what occurs behind the scenes before a recruiter calls you with an offer.

When a recruiter receives a job opening to fill, the hiring manager always lets her know how much money he has in his budget to hire this person. The hiring manager gives an absolute maximum amount and the *ideal* amount he wants to pay. The ideal amount is usually about $5K to $8K lower than the maximum salary. This can vary from role to role, but there is usually a small gap for me to work with when speaking to candidates.

This all depends on the position you are interviewing for, of course. I've hired for a few hourly wage roles for which the pay was $8 per hour, period. In certain cases, a recruiter does not have any wiggle room.

So here is what you should keep in mind: In most cases, we can negotiate - so *do it*.

Your negotiating power is different based on what type of applicant you are (this is not to be confused with some of the types of applicants mentioned in chapter 4). There are three different types of applicants in the offer stage: The Active (explained in chapter 4), the Passive (also explained in chapter four), and the Unemployed.

As mentioned before, I always talk about compensation on my very first call. I do this so that I can set expectations, and I don't want to waste your time if for some reason there is a big gap between your salary expectation and what my company is offering. I normally ask Active candidates what current wages are. (Remember, an Active candidate is someone who applied for a position I'm trying to fill.)

Here is the secret—boy, my peers are not going to be happy with me, but I'll tell you anyway. If I'm hiring for a role and I know the manager has it in his budget to pay $45K for this position and you tell me you are currently earning $30K, I will tell you the position pays $35K. This will give you a $5K increase in your salary to come join my company. You still get a bump in your pay, and I end up saving the company some money—everyone wins. If you currently earn $45K and the position only pays $45K, then unfortunately you will not be able to negotiate anything in that case.

Now, on the other hand, if I'm speaking to a Passive candidate (someone who I found and called out of the blue to see if she wanted to pursue a career at my company), I don't ask her first what she is earning. I "sell" the company and opportunity to her, let her know what the position pays, and then ask if that is within her expectations.

So keep in mind that if a recruiter comes to you and tries to sell you on her opportunity, *you* have the power. You have the ability to ask what the position pays before you tell the recruiter what you earn.

When I call someone I really want for a job, I will give her the maximum salary because I want her so badly for the role, and I need to make it appealing for her to leave her current company to come join mine. So keep in mind that if you are a Passive candidate, *make sure you negotiate*.

So this leaves those of you who are unemployed. Here is the honest-to-God truth: *You do not have much negotiating power*.

Regrettably, we know you are unemployed and not bringing in an income. This does not mean we are going to lowball you and not pay you for your experience, expertise, scope of responsibilities, and education. No, we will still pay you a fair wage based on industry standards; however, I can honestly say that you will not have much wiggle room to bargain for a higher salary. This is another reason, as stated in previous chapters, that you should *not* leave a job before you have another lined up. Not only will you have a gap in employment, but you will lose your negotiating power and possibly have to take a lower salary.

Now that I've identified the three types of applicants and how identifying which one you are will dictate your negotiating power, we can move on.

A candidate should never turn down my offer due to money. *You heard that correctly*.

As mentioned above, I discuss salary on my very first call with a candidate to make sure we are both on the same page in terms of compensation for the role. So, if we make it past the first call, we have both verbally agreed that if I were to extend you an offer, you would accept. I can honestly say that when a candidate turns down an offer due to salary, it infuriates me. I feel like the candidate lied to me, wasted my time, and misused my manager's time, and I can openly say that he or she made me look bad to my hiring manger and team.

The interview phase should never get down to an offer and a candidate decline for salary, period.

Let me explain this from a different perspective. Let's say you are the hiring manager and you just received an awesome candidate; her name is Lesley Jones. You spent an hour phone-interviewing Lesley and an hour interviewing her in the office, and your team has met her for a few hours of their time. You let the recruiter know that Lesley is everything you are looking for, and you would like to make her an offer and need her to start in two weeks. A day goes by, and you are getting her desk set up, putting together an onboarding and training plan, and are excited for her to start. You then get an e-mail from the recruiter saying, "I'm sorry, Lesley has graciously declined our offer."

What would your first question be to the recruiter?

Let me answer that for you, because this is the response I receive 100 percent of the time. You would say, "Why did she decline? I thought you cleared her salary and it was within the range we offered." By not accepting our offer, Lesley made the recruiter look extremely bad to the hiring manager; she also made herself look like a liar—both not good.

The moral of this rant is that you need to be honest with the recruiter about your salary expectations, and if she cannot meet your expectations, then *do not* continue the interview process.

I have candidates all the time who stop the interview process in the middle and let me know that they are thankful for the opportunity, but after carefully thinking about the salary, they realize they would not be able to take that amount at this time. I fully respect people who are honest and don't misuse my time. I also understand there are other reasons to decline an offer. After interviewing you may have realized the role and responsibilities no longer interested you, you may not have clicked well with the manager or the team you met, you may not like the long commute to the office, and so on. Those are all viable reasons beyond the salary that I understand. If this is the case, please reach out to the recruiter and express your concerns with her. I guarantee she will understand.

A good negotiator knows her value and can justify why she deserves a higher amount. Based on the information above, you now know that a recruiter may have some wiggle room with her offer. So why not ask? You already know they want you for the job, so you have nothing to lose. Now, this does not mean you should negotiate a crazy amount higher. A safe range to negotiate is anywhere from $2K to $5K above the original offer. Anything more than that is pushing your luck and may backfire.

If you are an Active candidate, do not try to negotiate anything higher than $7K higher than what you currently make or have made in your past. Remember, you came to me, so there must be a reason you are looking.

You should be happy with any amount higher than your current salary. Sometimes the amount could be equal to or less than your current income. In any case, you know this information up front in your initial phone conversation with the recruiter.

Also, be ready to justify why you feel you are worth more money now than what your current or past companies paid you. What skills have you gained? What things have you accomplished that make you worth more? Have you received a degree since you started at your current company? Have you received any new certifications? Have you attended any training programs or taken any classes to enhance your skills? If so, then great! Those are all reasons why I would pay you more than your current company does.

If you are a Passive candidate, you have more power to negotiate. You could safely negotiate about $3K to $10K higher than the original offer, but do not negotiate more than $10K higher than your current salary. You have the ability to secure a higher amount because you are happy at your current job, and by leaving, you are doing us a huge favor. Anything above $10K higher would be looked at as being greedy.

I feel the need to make another public service announcement on behalf of recruiters everywhere: *Do not get caught up on a couple thousand dollars in an offer.*

In other words, if you had in your mind that you wanted $35K, the recruiter extends $33K, you try to negotiate, and she stands firm on $33K, just accept it. In the scheme of things, $2K over the course of the year is equal to you taking home $123 per month less. What this means is you can't go out to dinner as often and you may not be able to buy as much Starbucks coffee. We can all cut back on some things in our lives, so $123 a month can be cut pretty easily. It's not worth losing a great opportunity over that amount of money.

Finally, let's say the worst-case scenario happens and you do not receive the offer. You receive a call or e-mail from the recruiter letting you know they have decided to pursue a stronger candidate for the role. This is your time to respond back thanking everyone for the opportunity. Be polite and professional. Let them know you are happy for the opportunity and would like to be considered for other roles in the future. Please don't take any of this personally, and don't get upset with the recruiter.

This is the time to show your maturity and ability to handle rejection. Nothing is more appalling than when I call candidates to turn them down and they give me an attitude, raise their voice, and clearly show me how upset they are. Please don't do that. Keep your relationship with the recruiter; you never know what else may open up in the future. Remember, I want to hire you, but at the end of the day I need to listen to the hiring manager and what is best for the business.

I've touched upon base-salary negotiating, but please do not get caught up on salary alone when considering an offer. It is extremely important to take into account the *entire* offer package.

The entire offer package is different per company but usually consists of health benefits, paid time off, a 401(k) plan, and sometimes stock options. Secondly, look at the opportunity in front of you. You cannot put a number value on opportunity, but career growth is another aspect to take into account when looking at an offer.

It kills me when people decline an offer based solely on base salary. Think about how much it costs you to have individual insurance for your family. Add that amount to your salary. Then, if the company offers you a company match on your 401(k), add that match to 6 percent of your salary, which is free money given to you for retirement. Finally, think about the opportunity you have at this company. Will you be in line for a promotion? Do you see career growth and stability? If so, then you must take that into consideration *on top* of the salary.

I had a candidate who declined an offer that was $5K higher than his current salary and was a great new position that we created just for him. He was so stuck on his salary that he did not see that he now had three weeks of paid time off to be with his family, our benefits were 30 percent cheaper than what he was paying at his current company, our stock options were going to provide him with an additional $20K in a four-year period, and his current company did not match his 401(k) contributions when ours did.

So yes, while the salary offered was only $5K more, in the scheme of things, he would have been better off financially, *and* he would have had a brighter future.

I tried to explain this to him until I felt like I was beating a dead horse, and he still did not get the message. When I informed the manager of the bad news, the manager responded by saying, "Wow; if he wasn't smart enough to see the whole package we were offering, then we don't want him working here anyway." It sounds brutal, but it's the truth. As a professional, you need to see the bigger picture and not be stuck on the base salary.

If you are looking to relocate to a different state, it is imperative to research the difference in the cost of living from one state or city to another.

I interview candidates who currently live in California. I'm interviewing them for positions in sunny Florida. As you can imagine, California is a lot more expensive than Florida. I'm always shocked when I speak to candidates about the salary difference between the two states and about their dissatisfaction with the difference. Be prepared to take a 38 percent salary decrease if you are going from California to Florida. This means that if you are earning $90K in California, you will earn $55,800 per year to live the same lifestyle in Florida.

It's troubling when candidates "ho and hum" about that fact. They fail to realize that everything in Florida is at least 38 percent cheaper than in California. As of this writing, gas in Florida costs $3.45 a gallon, whereas in California drivers are paying almost $5.00. So yes, you are earning less, but things cost you less as well. The housing market is also completely different in each state. This even goes for shorter relocations, so do your research first to see the difference in the cost of living before you speak to a recruiter in a different state.

I know I've made it clear that *if* the recruiter has done her job correctly *and* the candidate has been honest throughout the process, then a candidate should never decline an offer.

Conversely, I'm aware that things may happen and surprises may occur in your life and cause you to decide that the position is not the right move for you at the time. So you will end up declining the offer for various reasons, which is acceptable.

When you decline an offer, please do it over the phone, not in an e-mail. Make sure to thank the recruiter for her time and the opportunity. Then let her know why you are declining the offer. Please do not just e-mail the recruiter or ignore their calls. As mentioned before, I appreciate honesty and clear communication. So if you *must* decline an offer, keep in mind that you may be open to accepting at a later date, so don't burn your bridge.

As long as you have taken the correct approach and declined in a professional manner, I will have no problem reconsidering you in the future.

The offer stage can get pretty complex. Remember to have clear communication and make sure the recruiter is fully aware of your salary expectations from the very beginning. Take into account if you are an Active, Passive, or Unemployed candidate to know your negotiating power. And finally, consider the entire offer package; do not focus on salary alone.

By understanding this information, your offer should be an enjoyable and happy experience.

CHAPTER 13

WELCOME TO THE REAL WORLD

"How do I get experience when everyone is requiring experience?"

ALISSIA MCFARLINE, RECENT COLLEGE GRADUATE

I f you're a recent college graduate, still in college, pursuing college, or going straight from high school to work, this chapter is for you.

I'm confident that the question above has been relevant in your life at one point in time—maybe now. It's extremely unfortunate because many students listen to their career advisors, professors, coaches, and parents. I know that sounds odd; however, I've learned that much of the information provided by these individuals to their students and children is incorrect and only hurts them down the road. I'm not bashing *all* parents and educators because there are some great people out there helping guide young professionals through getting their careers up and running. However, I'm here today to set some things straight, and I hope everyone reading this chapter considers all I say carefully.

In the survey I conducted, I asked the recruiters the following question: "What percentage of your openings requires a bachelor's degree or some sort of higher education?"

The results were as expected. Only 10.9 percent said, "None."

This means that only 10.9 percent of the openings the recruiters are hiring for don't require a degree. So if you do not have some sort of higher education, you are losing out on more than 90 percent of job openings. So what does this mean to you? The information gathered shows the value of higher education. This also means that not only are you competing with those who have their college degrees, the pool of openings you are qualified for has drastically diminished.

To apply to 90 percent of the openings posted on the Internet, you must have some sort of education beyond high school. So now the real question comes into play: How do you get a job with a degree but no experience? Or how do you get experience without experience?

I'm going to break down the four different categories listed in the beginning of this chapter so that you can read what relates to your current situation.

HIGH SCHOOL-EDUCATED

There are many reasons why people go straight from high school to work and do not pursue a college education. I'm not here to question or judge you on making that decision. I'm confident you are now fully aware of the challenges you are facing due to this decision. People who do not have a degree need to focus on a trade or skill and master it. You cannot jump around from job to job and not focus on a specialty. I will be happy to hire someone who went straight from high school and focused 100 percent on a certain skill or trade and is an expert at it.

There are many jobs that do not require a bachelor's degree, such as the following (some of these require training or an associate's degree):

- Dental Hygienist
- Online Advertising Manager
- Web Developer
- Medical Secretary

- Paralegal Assistant
- Stenographer/Court Reporter
- Heating and Refrigeration Mechanic
- Surveyor
- Executive or Administrative Assistant
- Insurance Agent
- Industrial Machine Repairer
- Cosmetologist or Massage Therapist
- Hair Stylist
- Tax Examiner/Collector
- Wholesale Sales Representative or most sales positions
- Construction Machine Operator
- Electrical Technician
- Architectural Drafter
- Teacher's Aide
- Real Estate Agent
- Sewage Plant Operator
- Power Plant Operator
- Criminal Investigator
- Elevator Installer/Repairer
- Air Traffic Controller
- Nuclear Operator
- Radiation Therapist
- Commercial Airplane Pilot
- Loan Officer
- Firefighter
- Police Officer
- Mechanic
- Plumber
- Truck Driver
- Occupational Therapy Assistant

Most of these roles do require some sort of certification or an associate's degree, so if there is something you like on the list above, please do your research to see what steps you need to take to get where you want to go. Try to talk to people who are currently in the role you want. Ask them how they got there and what you need to do to get started. Take time to network with others, talk to your friends and family, and get out and connect with someone in that role.

When choosing a career path, remember what was mentioned in chapter two: Pick something that you love doing and are naturally good at. Don't pick something just based on income. Remember, if your job is something that you enjoy doing, you won't feel like you are working. That should be your ultimate goal, as opposed to making a lot of money.

Even without a college degree, you can make a good life for yourself. Focus on a trade or skill, take time to get the certification if it's needed, and master it.

CURRENT COLLEGE STUDENT

If you are currently enrolled in school and are pursuing an associate's degree or bachelor's degree, then this information is for you.

Here is the big issue I see with most college students: Their parents and friends have told them that their college years are meant to be full of hard work on their studies, but those years are also supposed to be the most fun of their entire lives. So this means you have two to four years to not work, party, and rack up debt. Then comes the day you graduate, and what do you think is going to happen? Do you think that debt will just go away? Do you think all of a sudden you will have a network of professionals in your field willing to help you find a job? Do you think you will have recruiters knocking at your door handing you a career? Do you think a company will invest $50K a year in salary for you just because you went to class, studied, and received a degree? Umm...nope!

I'm sorry to burst your bubble, but the reality is that college gives you two to four years to gain experience, network your butt off, and decide what it is you want to do with the rest of your life.

College is no joke, and that time should not be wasted with a lack of effort. What you do in those years is going to determine how quickly you become successful. I don't care if you received a full-ride scholarship; you cannot afford to lose the time you have while you are in school. What you need to realize at this very moment is that you have so many resources right now (explained below) that you won't have access to later, and you will need to use them to be successful when you graduate.

Last year, I received a LinkedIn request (LinkedIn requests are described in chapter eight) from a University of Central Florida student, Brian. I decided to accept him as a connection because I'm always willing to help college students, especially those who already know the importance of LinkedIn. After I accepted his connection, I received this follow-up e-mail from him:

> Hey, Alysse,
>
> Thanks so much for getting back to me so quickly. First of all, congratulations on your recent position as I see that you began working there in June, and I hope that you love it. With a proven track record in the industry, I would love to hear how you have been so successful and what you like about the industry.
>
> I would love to speak with you further either through e-mail, a phone call, or sitting down for lunch one day. Working as the Campus Representative for your company has been an amazing opportunity, and anything that I can do to get further involved would be great! Hopefully there is something I can do here at UCF to help you out.
>
> Please get back to me at your earliest convenience as I look forward to learning more from you.
>
> Thanks so much,
>
> Brian

I was so impressed with his ability to reach out to me and request a time to chat about *my* career. He was not asking about himself at all. He simply wanted to know how I liked my job and how I've become a success. How could I turn that down? I gave him a call, and after he asked me about fifteen questions (that I could tell he took the time to think about and write down) about what I do and how I got here, I then asked him about himself.

Brian informed me that he had always wanted to work at my company, so he connected with some people (using LinkedIn) at our headquarters in California and sold them on how they needed him to be a student representative on the UCF campus to help set up events and promotions for our new games that come out. They ended up agreeing, so for his entire junior year, he planned promotional events, advertised our products on a Facebook fan page, and became our official student representative on UCF's campus.

A few weeks before each product was released, my company sent him a bunch of cool giveaways, T-shirts, and promotional posters to hand out to the students. After each event, he had to send our corporate office a report as well as some pictures showing how successful the event ended up being. Brian did this for a whole year, and then I connected him with our university relations manager, who ended up hiring him for a marketing internship for a semester.

So by Brian's senior year, he already had more than a year and a half of marketing and sales experience before he even graduated. Not only did Brian have that experience under his belt, he was also an assistant brand ambassador for a company called Periscope, which held numerous college events on campus. On top of that, he also was an active member of the Professional Selling Program at UCF.

Needless to say, three months before he graduated, he had a job offer on the table and immediately accepted. I can honestly say I've never been more impressed by a college student before in my life. If I ever get the chance to meet his family, I'm going to ask them how they did such a great job raising such a professional young man.

You can all learn something from Brian. He's used his four years at UCF to network and be involved in groups and activities that UCF has to offer.

Here's the secret: When you are a college student, people are willing to help you out, so use it to your advantage. Use the time you have in college to network, network, and—did I mention?—network! Call up business owners and ask to meet with them to talk about their career.

Most colleges bring in guest speakers to talk about different topics. Not only should you attend these speeches, but stay after the presentation to shake the professional's hand and ask for a business card. After that, e-mail the speaker and request a time to chat further. Just like that, you've made a connection.

Connect with people who work at the companies where you want to work, and ask them if they can provide you with some advice or if they will meet you for a cup of coffee. Attend groups within your college that involve your area of focus. Not only should you be a member of different professional groups on campus, be a member of the boards of those groups, too.

There is a department at your college right now that can open hundreds of doors for you. The department is named something different at each school, but it's the career counseling department.

These departments are connected with hundreds of thousands of alumni who went to your school and are now working professionals. Go meet with a counselor and see if he or she can connect you with at least five alumni who do what you want to do. Then reach out to them. I guarantee you that alumni of your school will be more than happy to provide you with guidance or even an internship.

It's all about gaining connections and networking while you are in college, so use that department to your advantage. Once you graduate, they will no longer be able to assist you.

As discussed in chapter 2, it is important to do something you love to do. However, it's important to choose a major where you will find a job once you graduate. Do your research prior to buckling down in a major. There are numerous websites and helpful studies on the Internet that will break down the most hirable majors.

In the survey I conducted, I asked the recruiters to tell me what positions they were currently hiring for. The results are below.

As you see, based on what the recruiters who completed the survey said, as well as the current economic status, the most in-demand positions are in information technology, sales, software engineering, marketing/communications, engineering, business analysis, management, health care, and Java development.

The least in-demand roles are in retail, licensed social work, hospitality, food and beverage services, collections, and architecture. If you are passionate about a job that is on the lower end of the graph, please continue to chase your dream; just keep in mind that finding employment once you graduate may be slightly more difficult for you than for those who majored in other areas.

If you are interested in something that is not listed on the graph, that just means the 101 recruiters who completed the survey were not hiring for that role; it doesn't mean there aren't *any* open positions out there.

This leads me to the topic of internships or co-ops. Some students think all they need is the required number of internships for their major or minor. Well, I'm here to tell you, your success should not be decided based on the minimum a college requires you to get a degree. You should get as many internships while in college as you physically can. If you are obtaining a four-year degree, I recommend three to four internships. I don't care if this means pushing your graduation date back.

At the end of the day, a graduation date does not mean anything to your current employer or to me. What matters to me is the experience you gained while in school. I also don't care if it took you four years or six years to graduate. So if you are offered an internship, take it!

If you cannot get an internship, then volunteer. Try to volunteer in a field you are interested in, but if that does not work, then volunteer anywhere. By volunteering, you are showing a recruiter that you were doing something with your college life. Also, by volunteering you will be able to meet many new people who may be able to help you get an internship or job upon graduation.

Here is another resource that is literally in front of your eyes. You look at these people many hours a week and don't even realize how much help they can be to your success. These people are your professors. That's right—your professors are professionals in the field you want to work in.

Most of them have either worked in the industry you want to be in, or still work there. I want you to meet with all of your professors at least once a month to discuss your progress in the class and to talk about who they know and how they can help you get an internship, volunteer opportunity, or a job upon graduation. I don't care if it makes you look like a loser; I'd rather have you look "uncool" while in school than unemployed when you graduate.

Your professors want to see you succeed, so ask them!

Another thing recruiters like to see is that you worked while in school. I'm not saying you have to be in the exact field you want to work in, but we like to see that you were doing something to sharpen your skills, learn how to be a professional, develop the discipline to go to work, and overall gain experience for your résumé. Try to get a job with a retail store, a restaurant, a cell phone company, a call center, a landscaping company, a ticket sales outlet, an event-planning company, or an office as an assistant. All of these jobs will give you on-the-job experience and will show us recruiters that you have been doing something besides partying and going to class.

If Brian's story did not resonate with you, maybe mine will.

Throughout high school *and* college, I was a babysitter for numerous families. When I babysat, I treated it like my own business. I had a Palm Pilot (no, I didn't have an iPhone calendar at that time) that kept track of my school schedule, extracurricular schedule, personal schedule, and babysitting jobs. When I babysat, I conducted myself in a professional manner with the parents, took care of the kids effectively, and left the house cleaner than it had been when I got there. I never had friends over and never used the families' phone for personal calls, nor did I do anything to jeopardize the families' trust in me. I treated my babysitting job as if it were my own business.

The best part about the families I babysat for is that they were all very well-off financially. All of the families' fathers either owned their own businesses or were high up in seniority in their companies. I was a junior at The Ohio State University at the time, and Goran Marich was the father of one of the families I babysat for. He was the president and CEO of a local mortgage broker in my hometown of Richfield, Ohio.

One day, when I was babysitting, I asked Goran about his company and if he had the ability to hire me as an intern for the semester. Without any hesitation, he said, "Yes, I would be happy to provide you with a marketing internship at my company." Boom! Just like that, I had an internship.

The internship was forty hours a week for twelve weeks, so I took the semester off, moved back home with my parents, and worked full-time. Within three weeks of the internship, Goran called me into his office and offered me a permanent position as his executive assistant. He said he needed someone to work under him whom he could trust and whom he could count on to do a good job for him. What better person for the job than me, whom he trusted with his children?

I immediately accepted and worked for him during the day. I transferred all of my credits to The University of Akron and took classes at night. Within two years, I was promoted to marketing coordinator and then recruiter. Two years later, I graduated with my Bachelor of Science degree with a focus in business and organizational communications and a minor in marketing, and was immediately recruited by a large bank, in Cleveland, Ohio.

So just like Brian, I spent the last two years of my college life networking, interning, and working. When I graduated, I immediately had a job offer and have been employed ever since. I look back at my peers at the time who did not think about their careers while in college. They chose to stay out all night, sleep all day, and not network, and now they are paying for it.

I'm currently twenty-nine years old and have exactly nine years of corporate recruiting experience. I have accomplished so much as a young professional. I can only imagine where Brian will be when he is twenty-nine—probably running his own successful company somewhere, making a six-figure salary.

At this rate, where do you think you will be?

You have the time *now* to make some serious changes. Now is the time to be mature and get your life up and running. Do not wait until you graduate from college. I'm sorry to say it, but you live in a horrible time with the economy in shambles and unemployment at an all-time high. When you graduate, you are already too late. So it's even more important now than ever before to be proactive and get a jump-start on your career while you can.

These are the days when you need to buckle down, grow up, and be serious about your life. Once you receive that degree, you are in the boat with millions of other new graduates all fighting for the same jobs.

Resources that were so easily handed to you while in college will be no longer available, so don't waste them. You are paying thousands of dollars of either your money, your parents' money, or the school's money, so use every dollar to help you get a career.

THE RECENT COLLEGE GRADUATE

I'm going to start off by saying congratulations! I'm sure you are so excited to enter the real world—or maybe you are a little scared. Being scared is normal, and you honestly *should* be scared.

I'm here to make this a less-scary process. This book is providing you with an arsenal of tips and secrets that I hope you think about and act on. Recent college graduates, aka RCGs, are one the most confused and misinformed groups of applicants I work with. If you take everything I say in this book seriously, you will not become one those people. You will set yourself above the other RCGs.

If you have already graduated and did not follow my advice for the college student above and did not receive any sort of internship or work experience while in school, then you don't have the ability to be picky about what you do now. I'm sorry to say this, but at this time you just have to get someone to believe in your potential and hire you to give you experience.

The first thing you need to do, if you have not already done so, is get on LinkedIn. Follow my advice in chapter eight about how to set up a LinkedIn account. Next, set up an appointment with the career services department at your college and get a list of alumni who currently work in your field. Next, link up with them on LinkedIn and/or e-mail them to see if they have time for you.

I'm aware that this is easier said than done, so you need to tap into your network of friends and family immediately. Network with the people you know, and see who they know. Start to network immediately. Don't just sit around and apply for jobs online; that is *not* the best way to gain employment.

Next, once you start to talk to people, including recruiters, don't even take compensation into consideration when looking for work. I'm sorry to tell you this, but just because you have a degree does not justify an immediate $50K-a-year salary. You may have to take a something that pays $25K and work your way up, like everyone else. The degree you earned allowed you to be qualified for the role above those who do not have the degree. Now, once you get the job and work hard at it for years, you will see your salary rise.

As mentioned in chapter twelve, during the interviewing stage, you have *zero* negotiating power. You have little to no experience, so we are not going to pay you for what you can bring to the table other than potential. You will need to prove to a company what you are capable of before its hiring managers will offer you a high salary. So roll your sleeves up and get ready to work.

At the end of the survey I conducted, I asked the recruiters to provide me with their advice for current college students or recent graduates. There are a lot of quotes here, but I feel that this is especially important for you to read and let sink in. After all, your college education was a huge investment, so I'm here to show you how to get some return on that investment.

The quotes below deal with many things however the common thread is to take action! No one is going to do it for you, not your mother, father, boyfriend, girlfriend, manager, or siblings. You are your own best (or worst) friend, so get out there and start making things happen. Once you do, you will begin to unleash your potential and opportunities are sure to follow.

- "Always follow up with a letter after interviews. It shows initiative and professionalism."
- "Find companies looking to hire new college graduates. Get a foot in the door."
- "Take a job in your field of study so you can continue to learn."

- "Intern, use LinkedIn for alumni at solid companies—use all school resources and network, network."
- "Put down all volunteer work and make sure that it's very clear and is applicable to the position that you are applying for."
- "[Prepare a] detailed résumé with all externship/internship/volunteer experiences."
- "Keep an open mind and go on every interview you can."
- "Get any job you can to start your business experience."
- "Include a career summary with the title or functional area you are seeking, and then highlight your skills and accomplishments in a separate section that supports the stated summary. Put education at the end; that makes you look more professional than a recent grad."
- "Get as many internships or co-ops as possible."
- "Determine a career path and build your résumé around your chosen career. Try not to jump around from different job types—go for consistency."
- "Look at your first job(s) as an investment in yourself."
- "Communication is key. Don't ignore recruiters or not return phone calls. Don't lie on your résumé; most of the time we can tell."
- "Be ready to work at getting a job, and be realistic."
- "Get as much experience as possible!"
- "Get an internship during school!"
- "Volunteer, do internships…whatever it takes to show you have initiative."
- "Have a polished résumé and showcase good communication skills."
- "Ditch the résumé advice your career center gave you, and tailor your résumé for each position you are applying for, with as many examples to their requirements as possible."
- "Have realistic salary expectations. An education and no experience is great, but it doesn't mean that you should get $80,000. Also, I'd tell you to have a realistic view of your abilities. I think you need to balance education with as much experience as you can get. Once you get that experience, work hard and don't take an office environment for granted."
- "Understand that you need to start at the bottom, setting your expectations accordingly. Majoring in 'Business Management'

doesn't mean you will walk into a management role. Understand the compensation that you are seeking will most likely not meet market pay scales."

- "Do an internship before graduating. Do personal projects. Show your passion."
- "Make sure to have your correct contact information on your résumé so an employer can easily contact you about opportunities."
- "Start off with the jobs you like, because if you find that it's not for you, then you have time to change things up…Don't wait 'til you're older and hate your job and everyone around you."
- "Have passion for what you want to do, and bring that passion with you to interviews."
- "Find something way more fulfilling to do with your life."
- "Do internships or projects, and have realistic expectations on salary and working your way up."
- "Network and become active in the community."
- "Highlight relevant experience in your college/extracurricular activities."
- "Do internships and projects to keep your skills honed. Don't take a job out of your area of expertise just to pay the bills; it will pay off in the long run."
- "If you didn't do internships, put all of your relevant and hands-on experience and what you are looking for on your résumé, or go to companies and do an internship for six months and gain experience."
- "Make sure all of your contact info is there and correct. Grab the employer's attention!"
- "Be realistic in your salary and position expectations. Network, volunteer."
- "Take an offer of great experience versus chasing an offer of the most money…Pay your dues for first year or two to set yourself up on a much better track for career path/growth."
- "Co-op, internship as much as possible."
- "Do whatever it takes to get your foot in the door to get some experience, even if it means taking a lower-level role."
- "Do internships, even if they are free internships. Be sure to get one in a related field and do as much as you can to get basic

experience in the internship(s). You will end up working sooner than your classmates if you get related experience quickly."

- "Stop acting like you deserve the world on a platter, and learn what hard work is. Get off your phone while you're at work, and stop posting ridiculous pictures all over Facebook."
- "Get an internship or some type of entry-level experience."
- "Get an entry-level position at an organization where your desired position is, and work your way up."
- "Network as much as possible, then leverage that network to search for opportunities. Write a very strong résumé, and take as many internship opportunities as possible."
- "Network, connect with recruiters at the companies that interest you, and don't give up!"
- "Research the organization prior to interview calls."
- "Find a company that you would like to have a career with and try to get your foot in the door, even if the position isn't exactly what you would like to do long-term....Prove yourself, and other opportunities should present themselves!"
- "Have realistic expectations. Start in an entry-level position within an industry/field you are looking to work in long-term. Remember, it is always about who you are up against when inter-viewing for a job."
- "Be humble and willing to work your way up."
- "Do internships, volunteer, attend functions to meet people, uti-lize alumni associations to meet people, and take risks."
- "Start volunteering to work at companies while still in school. Network with local HR professionals."
- "Be open to many experiences. Don't expect to graduate and make $100,000 and have a corner office right out of the gate."
- "Focus on parts of your education or extracurricular experience that have helped you attain the skills necessary for a job."
- "If you want sales, go to work for a F500 company and cold-call your butt off."
- "Network—100 percent."
- "Make sure that you list all of your community and club activi-ties, etc. Do a lot of volunteer work."

- "Work on as many projects as you can in your spare time; take freelance jobs…anything that can build your experience/skill set and give you something to show on a résumé and in an interview."
- "1. Network as much as you can with friends and family for career opportunities. I'd recommend LinkedIn as a great tool, or other social media channels. Announce on your Facebook account that you're graduating soon, or that you just graduated, and would appreciate any leads to career opportunities. 2. Google or research companies via LinkedIn that interest you, and reach out to the company's recruiters or the manager/director of the business unit you're seeking to join to introduce yourself. You must take initiative. Keep in mind you may need to lower your salary expectations to get your foot in the door, and then you prove yourself. Don't sell yourself short on salary, but be reasonable about it if it's a company you really desire to work and grow with."
- "Pull relevant experience from class projects or internships if you have them. You most likely also have relevant skills and experience from part-time or college jobs that you can show employers. Use your free time wisely. Get involved in clubs or workshops surrounding your area of interest and start networking."
- "Understand that you need to start in an applicable role and not think that you can come into the workforce ready to climb the corporate ladder ASAP. With that, compensation should be viewed accordingly."
- "Realize you are competing with a ton of people that have more experience than you. To get to your career goal, you very well may have to start in a job that you feel overqualified for. If you find a job that is in the industry or company you want to work for, take that entry-level position and kill it. Be passionate and dedicated. Employers can't help but love that enthusiasm, and it will get you promoted before you know it while you gain the experience you need."
- "Gain work experience wherever possible, and network using professional applications to ask for guidance and possible opportunities."
- "To put yourself out there, make sure you stay active on LinkedIn and the job boards, and make as many connections as you can.

The job world today is all about whom you know and the good impressions you make."

- "Research target companies. Call potential hiring managers directly. Aggressively make connections with target companies. Use LinkedIn to establish industry connections, but do it with an invitation to connect with a phone call, not just the 'LinkedIn' connection."

- "Don't wait for 'THE' Job to fall into your lap. Try and follow up with a phone call after you apply for a position. Never give up; it's a tough market, but you will find your game eventually!"

- "With the company I work for, my advice is to get your foot in the door. Work your way up. Our company values their employees and appreciates hard work. Hard work does not go unnoticed. We are also very big on internal opportunities/advancement. I always use myself as an example. I started with this company at an entry-level position and have worked my way up to a specialist-level position. It is usually very encouraging to new graduates with little work experience. I have watched it happen with my own eyes."

- "Be flexible with opportunities, even if it's not the most desirable position in regards to pay/hours, etc. If it's with a good company that can get you the experience you need to move up, go after the opportunity. Do not expect to be paid over $30k without a specific degree in engineering, etc. Everyone has to start somewhere!"

- "Look into working with a new college grad or intern program through larger companies in the industries you're interested in."

CHAPTER 14

MISSION IMPOSSIBLE JUST BECAME POSSIBLE

"After six months of trying to gain employment, I was ready to throw in the towel and apply for government assistance. Just as I was downloading the paperwork, I received a call from a recruiter and she extended me a job offer. If I can do it, so can you!"

ANONYMOUS, JOB SEEKER

I hope that by reading this book, you are getting a sense of confidence and faith that you can get a job.

I've opened up a whole new world to you and provided you with many tips and secrets about the gatekeepers who stand between you and your new career. By understanding what a recruiter *really* thinks, you should be able to win at the game of getting a job.

Before you play that championship game, though, you must practice first. So before you start to apply to openings, you now know that there are a bunch of things you must do to get yourself in game-day shape on a personal level. Make sure you have a clear understanding of your natural strengths and have a solid career goal, create a list of companies you want to work for, ensure that your social media pages are polished and professional, and increase your exposure to the world by networking your bottom off.

Whether you are currently enrolled in school, a recent college graduate, or a seasoned professional, finding employment is a complex process that is broken down into these stages: résumé writing, applying, phone interviewing, on-site interviewing, follow-up, and offer. By understanding how to perform at each level, you will be able to navigate the process more smoothly.

Throughout this book, I've provided results from a survey I conducted among 101 of my peers. I wanted to make sure you were receiving the most accurate, up-to-date and candid responses from recruiters across the nation. After all, my goal for writing this book is to unleash what is going on in a recruiter's mind.

My final request to the recruiters was: "Please provide any advice you have for the unemployed."

Some of the comments have been listed in other parts of this book, but I wanted to make sure that no comments or valuable advice were left behind, so I'm including the remaining comments below. I expect that you now feel like you have unlocked a secret society of information and can use that information to create your best life possible.

Now, go out and get that dream job of yours. You can do it!

Advice to the unemployed provided by the 101 recruiters who completed the survey:

- "Do not mass-blast your résumé to any opening. Tailor it to each specific opening where you have that experience. When a recruiter sees you blast to every job they or the company have posted, they are reluctant to call you, as it shows a lack of respect to the hiring partners and a lack of attention to detail."
- "Always conduct yourself with professionalism while in the interview process."
- "Go the extra mile to get consideration for qualified opportunities."
- "Every day is a *new* day. You will survive, and we can hear and smell desperation."

- "Don't make it sound like you are looking for a job when a lot of the time you are only wasting time."
- "Don't give up. Be persistent in your search; make sure your résumé speaks to the position you are applying for."
- "Take any job. Some money is better than no money."
- "Sign up with temp agencies that handle your field of work and accept assignments, then work them as if they were your dream job!"
- "Be positive. No matter how discouraged you are, do not share that with potential employers."
- "There are plenty of jobs. You need to ask yourself, do you want to be not working at $80k a year, or do you want to be working at $45k with full benefits? Not that I'm suggesting that people need to take that kind of cut in pay, but this thought process helps people face the realities of the marketplace and possibly open avenues they might not have considered."
- "A significant gap in employment can make employers think there is an issue. Always find legitimate ways to keep your résumé active, like volunteering or self-employment."
- "Present a clean résumé and have a good personality. Always dress to impress."
- "It takes a lot of hustle and persistence."
- "A good portion of people gain employment by who they know. If you don't have connections, take the time to research and tailor both your résumé and your cover letter to target companies."
- "Practice interviewing."
- "If you have not done so already, hire someone to professionally write your résumé. It will pay dividends."
- "Don't leave any company unless you have an offer in hand to join elsewhere."
- "Show how your skills are cross-functional and that you are a quick learner."
- "Each job is different, so be sure your résumé matches each one specifically. Yes, it's more work, but it will yield better results."
- "Great personality means that even if I can't get you this job, I'll keep you in mind for future roles (you don't even have to ask me!). A bad personality and attitude means I will tell other recruiters and hiring managers that I had a bad experience with

you. Getting the job is a huge achievement, but once you get the job, the hard part starts *now*. Not only do you have to figure out how to work in a corporate environment (any and all businesses should be considered corporate); you need to learn how to communicate effectively, speak effectively, and influence people—these are the traits that will help you move up. It's about what you do after the interview as well."

- "Network, network, network. Simply responding to a job posting is not enough. Find someone in the company and network with them."

- "Network with everyone—LinkedIn and personal networks and professional groups."

- "Don't have a negative attitude when looking for work. When I talk to people and they tell me how it is so hard out there, they are not getting hired because of their age, etc.,—this is a major turnoff! Always have a positive attitude when speaking with recruiters."

- "Making it easy for an employer to see how your skills and experience match with the position you are applying for will get you a much quicker response. Don't be general on your résumé and cover letter. Submit a cover letter with your application, even if it is just a short paragraph."

- "Get out there and find something that you like, and work hard at making it work for you."

- "Be open to reinventing yourself. Do not call the recruiter more than once a day."

- "Acting desperate is a big red flag. You have to convey that you want the job you are applying for, not just any job."

- "Have multiple résumés that target specific skills that would cater to various jobs."

- "Keep up on your knowledge; if the market is bad, go back to school and stay hands-on."

- "Repost your résumé every few days on career sites. Make your résumé 'easy on the eyes,' not too long, and use bullet points to describe your responsibilities."

- "Volunteer to show that you are doing something other than sitting at home. Put that experience on your résumé. Get LinkedIn."

- "Be proactive and network. Utilize social networking. Don't rely on job boards...don't just apply/submit a résumé and pray."
- "Be more flexible on salary. The most important goal is to get back into the workforce."
- "Ensure the résumé meets the requirements of the job you are seeking."
- "Get working on something that can relate back to your career. There are many options open to you other than just sending your résumé out to jobs."
- "Please don't send your résumé and then follow up with a phone call, thinking it's going to make you stand out—because it's not, and it only annoys me. You will find a job, so stay positive—recruiters can tell when you're disgruntled, and it's a major turnoff."
- "Be honest about what you know and honest about what you don't know. Lying will get you nowhere."
- "Apply for positions that you are interested in and that you meet the qualifications for."
- "Don't go over one year of being unemployed. The more of a gap, the harder it is for the third-party recruiting firm to help. This is not a good idea since third-party recruiting firms can probably get your résumé in front of a hiring manager more effectively than applying on your own can."
- "Make finding a job a full-time job."
- "Don't be afraid to use your network or to reach out to a recruiter directly. It shows initiative."
- "Unemployment occurs, especially in this economy. Potential employers understand that, but most companies still desire those who have been unemployed to be either pursuing education or professional training/development while looking for new positions."
- "Have a game plan and follow up on all résumé submittals to show your eagerness to join their team."
- "Working somewhere related to the field you are interested in is better than not working at all. It shows you will do the hard work to get to where you want to go."
- "Network and keep your skills sharp."

- "Do something—school, contract work, volunteerism—rather than just job search for too long a period of time."
- "Hit the pavement and network/stay active in job search. When you do find a position, stick around and show loyalty, as opposed to jumping ship frequently."
- "Keep your résumé updated."
- "Be aggressive, take risks, and just be honest. If you are enthusiastic, passionate, and excited, the interviewer will love you."
- "Get a job as close to your career goal as possible."
- "You have a better chance of getting a job through your network than most anywhere else unless you are in the top 10 percent at your past company; then recruiters will be calling you."
- "Find consulting/contracting work."
- "Be confident and be yourself. Pre-rehearse your interview answers with someone else or in front of a mirror. Always, dress professionally, smile, and give a lot of eye contact."
- "Target the companies and industries you are passionate about; 80 percent of the interview is personality fit."
- "Remember to have a niche; no one cares about the jack-of-all trades and being a master of none. Make sure you have updated skills that are relevant in today's market. Regarding technology, remove old technology software/hardware skills from your résumé, as they most likely have not been used or have been replaced by mobile. Keep your skills current and take project-management courses, as they are always helpful, and they can help you brush up on public speaking and preparing presentations."
- "It's a numbers game, so the more you put into finding employment the more success you should have."
- "Be able to show that you were doing something productive with your downtime."
- "List your skill set clearly on your résumé, along with projects and experience. The more clear and straightforward, the better."
- "Don't just apply to job postings via your normal job banks. Take initiative and reach out to personnel in those companies, which you typically can find on LinkedIn. Create a LinkedIn profile and use all the keywords that identify your skills. Make sure you dress for success on your first interview and follow up accordingly with

a thank you e-mail. A firm handshake, good eye contact, and good manners go a long way, too."

- "Stay on top of your skills—use your free time wisely to work on projects related to your field. Don't just apply online and leave it to fate; focus on building relationships through networking events, LinkedIn, etc. so you don't get lost in a black hole of resumes."

- "Don't give up your search. If you are persistent and leverage all of your resources you will land a job."

- "Use the job description to customize your résumé for every position. It is a must!"

- "No one actively calls up hiring managers within a company asking to be referred to a recruiter. No one actively calls up hiring managers to gather information about a company and their hiring projections. Job seekers are far too passive in their job searches. The sooner a job seeker determines the position or company isn't a match, the sooner a job seeker writes it off his or her list of potential employers."

- "Always do a follow up call; your application could be in the spam folder."

- "Be open to change! Think about relocating, or going to night school or trade school to learn subtleties of industry."

- "Have a positive mental attitude. Never get discouraged or give up on opportunities that are out there waiting to be discovered. You never know what someone might see in you—especially if you are full of personality and a great attitude! Smile always. Come to interviews dressed to make a great first impression, no matter what the position is you are being interviewed for. Do not chew gum in your interview, and turn your phone off."

Keep in mind, Recruiters are the gatekeepers between you and your future employer. By understanding how to get through that gate, you have dramatically increased your prospects of landing not just any job, but your dream job.

Use this information in *The Recruiting Snitch* to find the success you are looking for. When things look negative or are not working out the way you hoped, re-read the chapter(s) that relate to your situation for clues you may have missed or forgotten.

Remember, we want to hire you, and I want you to get hired. I wrote this book for you. I know it will help you succeed so long as you are willing to help yourself.

Here's to your success!